AN INTERMEDIATE
ENGLISH PRACTICE BOOK

KEY TO THE EXERCISES

AN
INTERMEDIATE ENGLISH
PRACTICE BOOK

KEY TO THE EXERCISES

S. PIT CORDER

LONGMAN

LONGMAN GROUP LIMITED

Longman House
Burnt Mill, Harlow, Essex.

First published 1960
Second impression 1961
*New impressions *1964; *1965; *1966;*
*1967; *1969; *1970; *1971;*
*1973; *1975; *1976 ;
*1978; *1979; *1981

ISBN 0 582 52513 6

Printed in Hong Kong by
Sing Cheong Printing Co Ltd

KEY TO THE EXERCISES

SECTION 1. ARTICLES AND POSSESSIVES

EXERCISE 1

1 Industry; The industry of Sheffield. 2 Modern literature; The literature of the XVIII century. 3 Ignorance; The ignorance of these people. 4 Beauty; The beauty of the night. 5 The intelligence of these children; Intelligence. 6 Public education; The education of little children. 7 Accuracy; The accuracy of your calculations. 8 Theft, murder and arson; The murder of his sweetheart. 9 Responsibility; The responsibility for providing the drinks. 10 Life; The life of these insects.

EXERCISE 2

1 Games; The Olympic Games. 2 The cats I breed; Cats. 3 Sewing-machines; The sewing-machine you lent me. 4 Grass; The grass in the valley. 5 Money; The money I gave you. 6 Oxygen; The oxygen in the air. 7 Water; The water in that basin. 8 The air we breathe; . . . of oxygen and nitrogen. 9 Pianos; The pianos they build . . . 10 Butter; The butter on your plate. 11 The paint I put on yesterday . . .; Paint. 12 Rubber and leather; The leather he uses . . .

EXERCISE 3

1 . . . I can tell you his wife's. 2 St. Paul's is the finest . . . 3 . . . please call at the butcher's. 4 . . . and some of Thackeray's. 5 . . . and that is my sister's. 6 . . . and not the cyclist's. 7 I think it is John's. 8 . . . but not Beethoven's. 9 . . . but not its captain's. 10 . . . much more stylish than Tom's. 11 . . . at the tobacconist's round the corner. 12 . . . at his uncle's. 13 She prefers my work to my brother's. 14 . . . not your employer's. 15 . . . where did you put Mary's.

EXERCISE 4

1 It is a habit of mine . . . 2 It was a favourite expression of my father's. 3 It is a weakness of Mary's to eat . . . 4 I see that a colleague of yours has had . . . 5 A neighbour of ours has . . . 6 . . . that some acquaintances of the Jones's have been . . . 7 Any idea of yours would be welcome. 8 . . . a book of Graham Green's about Mexico. 9 . . . I want to see one of yours. 10 That was a good suggestion of yours.

EXERCISE 5

1 That car of Robert's . . . 2 What about those plans of yours? 3 Can you remember that picture of Turner's . . .? 4 That brother of yours . . . 5 Those drawings of your son's . . . 6 I wish that servant of Mary's wouldn't . . . 7 These new shoes of mine . . . 8 . . . those keys of mine? 9 This latest hobby of John's . . . 10 Take away that beastly dog of yours. 11 . . . that new shop of the butcher's is . . . 12 That new teacher of the children's is . . . 13 . . . to hear that new radio of the Jones's. 14 Have you read that latest book of Waugh's. 15 . . . those old plans of yours?

Note: 'This' may be substituted for 'that' and 'these' for 'those' in all the examples in this exercise.

SECTION 2. SOME AUXILIARIES AND ANOMALOUS VERBS

EXERCISE 6

1 John could visit his club . . . 2 She said I could go . . . 3 Mary was able to cook . . . 4 We were able to see . . . 5 He was able to play . . . 6 His son was able to do arithmetic . . . 7 He could borrow the money . . . 8 She said they could come . . . 9 He agreed that they could drive the car . . . 10 I'm sure that they weren't able to understand . . . 11 Mother said that we could play in the garden. 12 They couldn't talk to each other . . . 13 They weren't able to talk . . . 14 They were able to buy a new car . . . 15 My father said we could buy . . .

EXERCISE 7

1 She managed to read Othello in class last night in spite of being a foreigner. 2 They managed to reach . . . Etc.

EXERCISE 8

1 She succeeded in reading Othello last night in spite of being . . . OR She was able to read Othello last night in spite of being . . .

EXERCISE 9

1 Little Willie can be very annoying . . . 2 This drug can be very useful . . . 3 John can be quite amusing. 4 It can be quite wet here . . . 5 The advice of one's friends can be quite useful. 6 It can be very dangerous to touch this animal. 7 Mr. Jones can be very angry with his

children. 8 My grandmother could be very strict . . . 9 It can be quite hot in this room . . . 10 He told me that Mary could be very rude. 11 It can be very boring to listen . . . 12 All of us can be forgetful. 13 . . . that bull can be very nasty. 14 Knowing a foreign language can be of great value. 15 Smoking too much can be bad for the health.

EXERCISE 10

1 They needn't send the letter . . . 2 We daren't light a fire . . . 3 Need you really be so rude . . .? 4 Dare he show himself . . .? 5 They daren't take the exam. 6 They needn't tell him . . ., need they? 7 Why daren't you keep . . .? 8 I needn't tell you . . . 9 How dare you say . . .? 10 Need I bring . . .? 11 . . . that he daren't wait for them. 12 John needn't cash the cheque . . ., need he? 13 She daren't usually ask him, dare she? 14 We needn't explain it all again, need we? 15 You daren't challenge me, dare you? 16 Mary needn't usually get up so early . . . 17 . . . that they needn't do their homework. 18 She needn't finish the work today, need she? 19 You needn't really drive so fast, need you? 20 I bet you daren't pull his beard.

EXERCISE 11

1 I didn't need to put on . . . 2 We needn't have bought . . . 3 He didn't need to speak to her . . . 4 John needn't have telephoned Mary . . . 5 They didn't need to take the exam . . . 6 You needn't have gone there . . . 7 The class didn't need to repeat the exercise . . . 8 He didn't need to turn on the light . . . 9 I needn't have lent him the money . . . 10 I didn't need to wear my glasses . . . 11 We needn't have visited our aunt . . . 12 They didn't need to fetch . . . 13 He needn't have sold . . . 14 The children didn't need to go to bed . . . 15 You needn't have brought a coat . . .

EXERCISE 12

1 I needn't. 2 I mustn't. 3 I mustn't. 4 He mustn't. 5 She needn't. 6 We mustn't. 7 We mustn't. 8 I needn't. 9 I mustn't. 10 They mustn't. 11 We needn't. 12 We needn't. 13 He mustn't. 14 I mustn't. 15 I needn't. 16 I mustn't. 17 He mustn't. 18 I needn't. 19 I mustn't. 20 I needn't.

EXERCISE 13

1 You needn't . . . 2 They mustn't . . . 3 John mustn't . . . 4 You mustn't . . . 5 You needn't . . . 6 You needn't . . . 7 . . . I mustn't . . . 8 . . . I needn't . . . 9 The children mustn't . . . 10 The children needn't . . . 11 You mustn't . . . 12 I needn't . . . 13 I mustn't tell . . . 14 He mustn't . . . 15 You needn't . . .

EXERCISE 14

1 That mountain must be ... 2 You must live about ten miles away.
3 These ruins must be ... 4 Mr. Smith must be a rich man ... 5
Those children over there must be playing ... 6 You must be mis-
taken. 7 The chickens must have been stolen ... 8 John must have
been working late. 9 You must have been very careless ... 10 He
must have been very busy ... 11 The examination must have been
very difficult ... 12 It must be going to rain. 13 They must all be
going ... 14 That must be Mrs. Smith ... 15 The children must have
had their dinner ... 16 I must have been dreaming when ... 17 The
Jones family must have gone ... 18 You must be mad to do that.

EXERCISE 15

1 Whether I shall ever ... 2 ... you shall have ... 3 Nobody shall
... 4 You shall ... 5 None of you shall leave ... 6 I will not ...
7 Will you lend ...? You shall have ... 8 I will agree ... 9 You shall
not ... 10 ... but I shall stop ... 11 I will go ... 12 That they
shall ... 13 ... he will ... 14 ... you will not like what I am ...
15 I shall be ... 16 ... shall die. 17 You shall go ... 18 Will you
do it, or shall I? 19 If you will ..., I will carry ... 20 ... we will not
... 21 You shall have ... 22 They shall not have ... 23 I shall
meet ... 24 I will meet ... 25 I shall not meet ... 26 I will not
meet you ...

EXERCISE 16

1 Shall we ...? 2 ..., shall I? 3 Will you ...? 4 ... will you? 5
Shall I ...? 6 Shall we ...? 7 ... shall we? 8 ... will you? 9 Shall
I ...? 10 ... shall we? 11 Will you ...? 12 ... will you? 13 Shall
I ...? 14 ... will you? 15 Shall we ...? 16 ... will you? 17 ...
shall I? 18 Will you ...? 19 ... shall we? 20 ... will you?

EXERCISE 17

1 I should ... 2 Would you ...? 3 ... she would ... 4 ... should
you ... 5 Would you ... 6 ... she should do. 7 ... it would be
... 8 ... they should have ... 9 What should it ...? 10 ... we
should ask ... 11 ... they would like ... 12 What would you ...?
13 Would you ...? 14 Dinner should be ... 15 ... he would have
to ... 16 ... they should ... 17 It should ... 18 To whom should
I ...? 19 ... the plane should land ... 20 ... the plane would
land ... 21 These things should not ... 22 ... they should all ...
and she would give ... 23 ... whether I should ... 24 ... they
should arrive ... 25 You really should not ... 26 ... he would
mind ...?

EXERCISE 18

1 John wishes his office staff would work ... 2 I wish you would answer ... 3 The police wish drivers would obey ... 4 The Headmistress wishes the girls would do ... 5 He wishes the dogs would stop ... 6 I wish everybody would be ... 7 Mary wishes John would smoke less. 8 Mrs. Jones wishes her maid would do ... 9 I wish you would not complain ... 10 The children wish their teacher would be ... 11 I wish you would try ... 12 The gardener wishes the dogs would keep ... 13 The people wish the government would do ... 14 The doctor wishes his patients would follow ... 15 Don't you wish the others would walk ...?

Note: 'I wish' may always be replaced by 'if only' in this exercise.

EXERCISE 19

1 They didn't have ... 2 He hasn't any money ... 3 He didn't have ... 4 They didn't have ... 5 They haven't seen anything ... 6 She didn't have ... 7 The children didn't have their ... 8 We didn't have ... 9 You haven't ... 10 I haven't ... 11 Has she anyone ...? 12 Did she have ...? 13 Did the judge have ...? 14 Does he usually have much ...? 15 Did she have ...? 16 Did John have ...? 17 Has February ...? 18 Had he any ...? 19 Has he anything the matter ...? 20 Did Mrs. Smith have ...?

EXERCISE 20

1 The children had a ride ... 2 ... let me have a look ... 3 I want to have a talk ... 4 Would you like to have a walk ... 5 We shall be having a swim ... 6 ... ought to have a sleep ... 7 ... and have a sail ... 8 I haven't had a drink of champagne ... 9 ... have been having a fight ... 10 ... wanted to have a smoke ... 11 ... he wanted to have a try. 12 Shall we have a dance? 13 ... need to have a wash. 14 They haven't had a quarrel ... 15 ... it would be best to have a lie down. 16 ... too cold to have a bathe. 17 ... generally have a rest ... 18 Have a taste and ... 19 ... had to have a sit down. 20 ... we must have a run through ...

EXERCISE 21

1 I am going to have my shoes mended. 2 They are going to get their new house designed by an architect. 3 ... to have her dress altered ... 4 ... of getting the grass cut. 5 ... I had my watch cleaned. 6 You really must get your eyes tested. 7 ... to have my car repainted ... 8 Can't you get the translation done? 9 See that you have your shoes cleaned ... 10 ... have the trees in his garden cut down. 11 ... the

Council are having the road mended. 12 . . . we must get our passports renewed by the Foreign Office. 13 Have you ever had your own voice recorded? 14 I hope you'll get the piano tuned . . . 15 . . . to have the children vaccinated.

SECTION 3. THE PASSIVE VOICE

EXERCISE 22

1 Children cannot be expected to understand . . . 2 The arrival of the next plane was announced . . . 3 It must be clearly understood that . . . 4 . . . that my car was decarbonized. 5 This mountain has never been climbed before. 6 Hopes have been expressed that . . . 7 . . . and he has not been seen again. 8 Were these vegetables grown . . .? 9 The Queen's Christmas message was heard . . . 10 His symphony was performed . . . 11 This exercise should have been checked . . . 12 All his calculations have been proved wrong. 13 It has been decided to open . . . 14 It cannot be denied that . . . 15 It must never be said that . . . 16 This piano has not been tuned . . . 17 Be prepared for the worst. 18 It cannot be helped if . . .

EXERCISE 23. For free completion.

EXERCISE 24

1 Mary was promised a new doll . . . 2 You will be given new instructions . . . 3 Were you sent the photographs you were promised? 4 The pupils have never been taught to do . . . 5 She was carefully shown how . . . 6 They were shown the house by the owner himself. 7 I was lent two priceless old volumes. 8 He was allowed five minutes . . . 9 She was asked her name . . . 10 The soldiers were told to . . . 11 I was told the latest news by a friend . . . 12 Have you ever been called a fool before? 13 She was recommended a new doctor. 14 John has been made manager . . . 15 Were you offered the job . . .? 16 Dr. Williams has been refused a visa by the consular authorities. 17 We were refused entry to the meeting . . . 18 I was ordered a new diet by the doctor. 19 The workers weren't paid the wages . . . 20 . . . when they were denied an opportunity of . . . 21 He was proved to be . . . 22 Were you given enough sugar? 23 Have you ever been asked to tell . . .? 24 I was most rudely answered . . . 25 I was offered a much higher salary . . . 26 J. Smith and Co. were appointed auditors . . . 27 Have you ever been refused a Life Insurance Policy by any other company?

28 I was never taught the rudiments . . . 29 Look what I have been given. 30 He must be told that he is not to . . .

EXERCISE 25

1 Look how well those children have been brought up. 2 These words should all be looked up . . . 3 Now that my mistakes have been pointed out to me . . . 4 This matter must be gone into. 5 . . . as all your words will be taken down. 6 This business has just been taken over by . . . 7 A rise in prices has been brought about by . . . 8 All those bad debts must be written off. 9 . . . he was run down by a bus. 10 She cannot be taken in so easily. 11 All my worst fears have been borne out by what has happened. 12 The bad radio reception was put down to the . . . 13 Have all the fireworks been let off yet? 14 I can't be caught out as . . . 15 The house was locked up . . . 16 Have all the dishes been washed up yet? 17 The money was shared out . . . 18 . . . that his instructions have been carried out.

SECTION 4. RELATIVE CLAUSES

EXERCISE 26

1 defining; 2 non-defining; 3 defining; 4 defining; 5 non-defining; 6 defining; 7 non-defining; 8 defining; 9 defining; 10 non-defining; 11 non-defining; 12 non-defining; 13 non-defining; 14 non-defining; 15 defining; 16 defining; 17 non-defining; 18 non-defining; 19 defining; 20 defining.

EXERCISE 27

1 that; 2 that; 3 that; 4 that; 5 which; 6 who; 7 that; 8 that; 9 that; 10 who(m); 11 whom; 12 that; 13 that; 14 that; 15 that; 16 that; 17 which; 18 that; 19 which; 20 that.

EXERCISE 28

1 ——; 2 which; 3 whom; 4 who; 5 who (that); 6 which; 7 ——; 8 ——; 9 ——; 10 who (that); 11 ——; 12 ——; 13 who (that); 14 that; 15 who; 16 who; 17 that (which); 18 ——; 19 which; 20 ——; 21 ——; 22 that; 23 that; 24 who (that); 25 ——; 26 ——; 27 which; 28 ——; 29 that (which); 30 ——.

EXERCISE 29

1 whose; 2 of which; 3 whose; 4 whose; 5 whose; 6 whose; 7 of which; 8 whose; 9 whose; 10 whose; 11 whose; 12 of which; 13 whose; 14 whose.

EXERCISE 30

1 These are the things I spoke about just now. 2 Here is a story I want to tell you. 3 Now do you see the point I was trying to make? 4 ... with a man she had never met before. 5 Here are the exercises you must do. 6 These are some flowers I have been trying to grow ... 7 This is a hill we tried to climb last year. 8 What is the word you want to look up? 9 Tobacco is a drug I can't do without. 10 ... the name of the book Joan was looking for? 11 Is that the dish you asked the waiter for? 12 ... on the pile you can see in front of you. 13 Is this the pen you have been trying to write with? 14 ... the sort of nonsense I won't put up with. 15 Is this the house you were born in? 16 Arabic is a language I find difficult to learn. 17 ... of the man you are getting married to? 18 Where are the papers you wished to show me? 19 ... the man you were telling me about? 20 ... the vegetables they sell in the market.

EXERCISE 31. For free completion.

EXERCISE 32

1 where; 2 why; 3 where; 4 where; 5 where; 6 when; 7 why; 8 where; 9 why; 10 when.

EXERCISE 33

1 ... which pleased her ... 2 ... which was extremely ... 3 ... which made his parents ... 4 ... which made everybody ... 5 ... which made her ... 6 ... for which I was ... 7 ... which didn't surprise me ... 8 ... which is, I think, ... 9 ... to which they replied ... 10 .... by which you can tell that they ...

EXERCISE 34

1 ... for what I can get. 2 ... about what you are going to do. 3 ... part of what I gave you. 4 After what has happened, ... 5 ... by what he does. 6 According to what they have ... 7 ... on what you mean. 8 What she tried to ... 9 ... with what he had ... 10 ... through what looked like ... 11 ... by what he thought must have been ... 12 Tell me what you propose. 13 What I don't understand is ... 14 Following on what you have just said ... 15 ... of what she has just done. 16 ... at what had happened. 17 ... irrelevant to

what we are discussing. 18 . . . to what he said yesterday. 19 . . . sorry
for what he has done.   20 . . . of what you think . . .

EXERCISE 35

1 wherever; 2 whoever; 3 whichever; 4 wherever; 5 to whoever;
6 of whatever; 7 whatever; 8 for whatever; 9 whoever; 10 whoever; 11 for whoever; 12 whatever; 13 with whoever; 14 whichever; 15 whichever; 16 from whoever; 17 whichever; 18 whichever; 19 wherever; 20 wherever.

SECTION 5. WORD ORDER

EXERCISE 36. As example.

EXERCISE 37

1 Did you hear what she said to her friend? Etc.

EXERCISE 38

1 It is a serious question whether . . . 2 It is incredible that he . . .
3 It still remains a mystery where he . . . 4 It seems very improbable
that he will . . . 5 It is easy to make fun of her, but it is cruel to do so.
6 It is not known what they . . . 7 It seems quite useless to try . . .
8 It would seem a very good idea in the circumstances to buy . . . 9 It
is generally considered most unwise to . . . 10 It has been found impossible to reach the top . . .

EXERCISE 39

1 To be wise after the event is perfectly easy. 2 To shake him by the
hand was a great experience. 3 To accept that responsibility is a very
serious matter. 4 That he has been most unwise is clear. 5 To hear
him speak French is quite a new thing for me. 6 To bring your own
towels . . . will be quite unnecessary for you. 7 To meet your sister has
been a great pleasure for me. 8 To build a wall so that . . . is by no
means easy. 9 To get married seemed the most natural thing in the
world. 10 To get them to stay proved quite impossible. 11 That they
will come appears very likely. 12 To see swallows in the . . . is most
unusual.

EXERCISE 40

1 It was only last week that I saw him . . . 2 It is the doctors who make . . . 3 No. It's my book I've lost. 4 It was in the park that we met them. 5 It's tonight (that) I hope to go to the theatre. 6 It is because you have lost all his papers that he is angry. 7 It's your brother (that) I want to talk to. 8 It was his gloves (that) he was looking for. 9 It was to go to the party that she bought a new dress. 10 It was later in the evening (that) he got lost. 11 It was five years ago that I first got to know them. 12 It was on her account that he made a fool of himself. 13 It was years later that I discovered . . . 14 It was by mistake (that) she gave him . . . 15 It was outside in the garden (that) she lost . . . 16 It is for your own good that you should . . . 17 It is you who are wrong, not me. 18 It was in order to teach him a lesson that we punished him. 19 It was a large pile of bricks that fell down . . . 20 It is since they came back, not before, that they have had . . .

EXERCISE 41

When was it (that) you met her . . .? 2 How long is it since we met? 3 What is it (that) he's looking for? 4 Why was it (that) he couldn't come? 5 What was it (that) he'd lost? 6 What is it you're waiting for? 7 Who was it (who) telephoned? 8 Where was it she died? 9 Why is it (that) he can't understand? 10 Whose fault was it (that) the vase got broken? 11 How long ago was it (that) he passed . . .? 12 When was it you saw them last? 13 What is it you don't understand? 14 Where was it (that) you studied Spanish? 15 Which was it (that) fell and got broken?

EXERCISE 42

1 Hardly had he finished his dinner when . . . 2 Little do you know of what . . . 3 Even less do you know of what . . . 4 Not only did he show her how . . . 5 Never in all my life have I seen . . . 6 Rarely has there been such a . . . 7 Nowhere could you find . . . 8 Only by chance did I hear that . . . 9 Seldom have we been treated . . . 10 At no time has it been easier to . . . 11 Only today did I learn the . . . 12 To such a degree did he become confused . . . 13 . . . and not till then did he learn that he . . . 14 To such an extent has the situation deteriorated that . . . 15 Not a sound did he make. 16 Not a word did they speak. 17 Nor could I make him see . . . 18 Nor would she do as . . .

EXERCISE 43

1 She very much enjoys dancing. OR She enjoys dancing very much. 2 He slowly turned to face . . . 3 I believe you deliberately did that. 4 . . . to be climbing the mountain at a snail's pace. 5 They gladly

went out to get some fresh air in the park. 6 They desperately tried to save . . . 7 I firmly believe they will come home today. 8 Then gently stir in the sugar. 9 He wrote an account of his life at sixty. 10 They were dancing together all last night. 11 Write these sentences in ink. 12 He carefully put the money away in his purse. 13 I distinctly heard a cry outside. 14 They thoughtlessly left their books at home. 15 I vaguely remember having heard . . . 16 We strongly dislike that food. 17 . . . entered the main road at ten miles an hour. 18 I will gladly lend you . . . 19 You can't possibly want . . . 20 You should carefully consider it . . . 21 He cautiously raised the lid with one hand. 22 You must definitely make up your mind tonight.

EXERCISE 44

1 We are still working . . . 2 They have not yet finished . . . 3 I have already told . . . 4 We had only just come in . . . 5 Her mother wholly approved . . . 6 I shall never believe . . . 7 You will scarcely have heard . . . 8 It cannot entirely be explained . . . 9 They were largely responsible . . . 10 Have you ever seen an octopus? I never have. 11 You can hardly excuse yourself . . . 12 I generally try to do . . . 13 He sometimes comes . . . 14 He little understands . . . 15 He would always have been . . . 16 It is by no means certain that . . . 17 I have rarely seen . . . 18 He is partially to blame . . . 19 I can to some extent understand . . . 20 She frequently stays . . .

EXERCISE 45

1 . . . working in this room all day. 2 He was born in Paris in 1943. 3 Take this to your mother immediately. 4 Look carefully at this sentence OR Look at this sentence carefully. 5 Come here immediately. 6 He has loved her fanatically all his life. 7 They were caught in the rain yesterday. 8 . . . your books quietly in the library. 9 They returned to their hotel with their friends at eleven o'clock. 10 He has been sitting quite quietly on that chair for ten minutes. 11 They came up to the fire a few minutes later. 12 The goalkeeper remained lazily in the goal-mouth all through the game. 13 He went upstairs to fetch his coat a few minutes ago. 14 The plane arrived early at the airport. 15 I shall meet you at the party this evening. 16 They are going to their parents for the week-end. 17 I said good-bye to them regretfully at the station yesterday. 18 Let's invite them to the theatre tonight. 19 I have been living quietly in Rome since 1942. 20 She spoke to him quietly in the hall after dinner.

Nos. 7, 9, 11, 15, 17, 19, can equally well have the adverb of time at the beginning.

A 2

EXERCISE 46

1 on the steps outside the town hall. 2 clearly and with deliberation.
3 on the left in the passage upstairs. 4 carefully with your right hand.
5 on the table in the dining room. 6 at six o'clock this morning. 7 very
high over Paris. 8 clearly and with a loud voice. 9 in the afternoon
on Thursday next week. 10 before midday tomorrow.

EXERCISE 47

1 It was firmly stuck . . . 2 . . . was well received. 3 It has been care-
lessly thrown away. 4 She has been completely restored . . . 5 He is
highly respected . . . 6 . . . has been seriously damaged. 7 It has been
sadly neglected. 8 It must be clearly understood. 9 . . . must be better
prepared. 10 The food was beautifully served.

EXERCISE 48

1 quiet well-ordered. 2 A delicious cup of hot China tea. 3 poor de-
fenceless. 4 fine old Tudor. 5 deep luxurious. 6 long boring technical.
7 useless old. 8 pale weak sick OR weak pale sick. 9 happy active
intelligent. 10 recent depressing. 11 nasty dirty industrial. 12 rude
lazy disobedient. 13 rich indigestible. 14 slow elderly incompetent
15 deep clear motionless. 16 delicate pink Japanese porcelain. 17
fantastic incredible ghost. 18 beautiful formal French. 19 fine old
carved oak. 20 attractive broad-brimmed Mexican.

EXERCISE 49

Note that, although the instructions say that you must put the adjectives
after the noun, in Nos. 4, 6, 8, 10, 12 it is equally correct to put them
before the noun.

EXERCISE 50

1 His numerous relations were all present . . . 2 The girls we met last
night both danced . . . 3 The exercises you have done so far are all too
easy. 4 The lights in the town were all out. 5 The beer we bought has
all been drunk. 6 I suppose the people . . . will all come . . . 7 The
letters . . . were both sent . . . 8 . . . when the children have all been
inspected. 9 The lights in the town all went out . . . 10 The lights in
the town have all gone out.

EXERCISE 51

1 . . . to know where you are going. 2 She wonders how often they
visit their friends. 3 Tell me what you mean. 4 Have you told her yet
how much you love her? 5 . . . explain to me how you perform this
operation. 6 . . . whether he can help her. 7 . . . told me yet when they

intend to leave. 8 ... whether he will undertake ... 9 I have no idea which you prefer. 10 He doesn't know why she never came. 11 ... whether she is married. 12 ... asked me what time the concert begins. 13 Tell me why you have disobeyed my orders.

SECTION 6. INFINITIVES AND GERUNDS

EXERCISE 52. As example.

EXERCISE 53. As example.

EXERCISE 54

1 Do you remember meeting her ...? 2 Please remember to wipe your feet ... 3 I completely forgot to lock the front door ... 4 Don't forget to bring ... 5 I shall never forget meeting ... 6 These stockings need mending. 7 Do you really need to buy ...? 8 We regret to inform you ... 9 I greatly regret having lent her ... 10 Do you remember meeting John ... 11 She has already forgotten lending him ... 12 Does your car need washing? I certainly need to wash mine. 13 ... you will regret having lent her ... 14 He's just trying to open the tin. 15 Just try to be a little more co-operative. 16 I have been learning skating ... 17 ... he learnt to write ... 18 ... I regret to say. 19 You should try using petrol ... 20 Try tasting it ...

EXERCISE 55. Free completion exercise.

EXERCISE 56

1 before making sure. 2 after being. 3 after eating. 4 while lying. 5 before disturbing. 6 on his turning. 7 on hearing OR after hearing. 8 after considering. 9 before putting. 10 before taking. 11 on hearing. 12 while returning. 13 while having. 14 after hearing. 15 while looking.

EXERCISE 57. Free completion exercise.

EXERCISE 58

1 They did too much drinking ... 2 John never does much gardening ... 3 ... the Jones sisters do a lot of dancing. 4 I do too little practising ... 5 ... I have to do a lot of writing. 6 Will you do much walking ...? 7 ... I want to do a lot of sight-seeing. 8 We used to

do a lot of running . . . 9 . . . ladies were all taught to do a little singing and painting. 10 . . . does too much talking. 11 I need to do a lot of travelling . . . 12 . . . does a lot of entertaining . . . 13 Do you do much fishing? 14 . . . I haven't done much listening-in. 15 . . . he did too much smoking. 16 . . . if he had done much flying lately.

EXERCISE 59. As example.

EXERCISE 60. Free completion exercise.

EXERCISE 61

1 The weather must not be allowed to . . . 2 I was tempted to try . . . 3 We were warned not to . . . 4 . . . everybody was obliged to . . . 5 Visitors are not permitted to . . . 6 They should be told to . . . 7 We were all taught to . . . 8 All the spectators were requested to . . . 9 He cannot be persuaded to . . . 10 We were all invited to . . .

EXERCISE 62

1 I guess that it is . . . 2 We estimate that it weighs . . . 3 Do you suppose that this exercise is . . . ? 4 Do you believe that it is possible . . . ? 5 We understand that he is . . . 6 . . . and found that it has . . . 7 . . . I see that it is . . . 8 . . . think that this invention has . . . 9 . . . consider that there is no . . . 10 . . . declared that the patient was . . .

EXERCISE 63

1 Mt. Everest is known to be . . . 2 The gold mine was estimated to have . . . 3 That book was believed to be . . . 4 Dr. Robinson is understood to be . . . 5 It was found to be too expensive . . . 6 The sun has been calculated to be . . . 7 It is generally considered to be . . . 8 The prisoner was declared to be . . . 9 The government policy was acknowledged to be . . . 10 George was reckoned to be . . .

EXERCISE 64. As example.

EXERCISE 65. As example.

EXERCISE 66. Free completion exercise.

EXERCISE 67. Free completion exercise.

EXERCISE 68. Free completion exercise.

EXERCISE 69

1 . . . was surprised to see them . . . 2 We are proud to announce . . .
3 . . . be pleased to deliver . . . 4 . . . was happy to be home . . .
5 . . . was angry to find that . . . 6 . . . amazed to hear . . . 7 . . .
shocked to hear . . . 8 . . . ashamed to appear . . . 9 . . . amazed to
hear . . . 10 . . . sad to hear . . . 11 . . . upset to learn . . . 12 . . .
overjoyed to see . . . 13 . . . glad to have . . . 14 . . . surprised to get
. . . 15 . . . delighted to receive . . .

EXERCISE 70

1 All children are to bring . . . 2 She told him he was to do . . . 3 . . .
all firms were to pay . . . 4 They are not to attempt . . . 5 . . . what
she was to do. 6 Passengers are to hand in . . . 7 All radios are to be
switched off . . . 8 . . . that he was never to speak to her . . . 9 No one
is to go . . . 10 . . . who they were to apply to . . . 11 How . . . are we
to overcome . . . ? 12 You are on no account to speak . . . 13 All
drivers are to show . . . 14 Where am I to take . . . ? 15 . . . that they
are not to let . . . 16 What is to be done . . . ? 17 . . . where all his
friends were to be found. 18 The meat is to be served first . . . 19 All
articles . . . are to be declared. 20 All papers are to be handed in . . .

EXERCISE 71

1 . . . for us to interfere . . . 2 . . . for them to pay . . . 3 For him to
play the piano . . . 4 . . . for the board to consider. 5 . . . something
for you to see. 6 . . . for all to inspect. 7 . . . for all the children to
have for tea. 8 Why did you choose that book for us to read? 9 . . .
for him to do! 10 . . . for her boy-friend to return. 11 . . . ready for
you to drive. 12 . . . too expensive for me to buy. 13 . . . for me to
correct . . . 14 . . . for the dog to come in. 15 . . . for the film to begin.
16 Are these shoes big enough for you to wear? 17 . . . not deep
enough for us to dive into. 18 . . . for them to identify there. 19 He
has arranged for them to look after his house . . . 20 Is the soup cool
enough for us to drink yet?

EXERCISE 72

1 Is there anything there to see? 2 . . . a man to trust. 3 . . . no one
to help me. 4 . . . a man to be trusted. 5 . . . anything to do. 6 . . .
anything to declare? 7 . . . There is a lot to be done. 8 . . . an occasion
not to be forgotten. 9 . . . no money left to spend. 10 . . . you have a
train to catch. 11 . . . a book to read . . . 12 . . . a hundred and
one things to be done. 13 . . . something to drink? 14 . . . someone
to carry her bags . . . 15 . . . somewhere to go . . . ?

EXERCISE 73. As example.

SECTION 7. TENSES OF THE VERB

EXERCISE 74

1 He came ... 2 We usually have ... 3 Water always freezes ...
4 Students frequently make ... 5 I have ... 6 I took ... 7 He
came ... 8 ... she wore ... 9 .... my car boils. 10 She sang ...
she doesn't sing .... 11 I seldom see ... He went ... 12 ... her
sister cooked ... 13 ... he says ... 14 ... he doesn't bother ...
15 ... I went ... 16 ... frequently fought ... seldom do. 17 How
often did you go ...? 18 Did you play ...? 19 ... built ... 20
... always gave me ... 21 ... a pianist practises ... 22 ... he lies
... 23 My aunt Jane hated ... 24 We all studied ... 25 Wood
always floats.

EXERCISE 75

1 ... usually run ... but today they are not running ... 2 John
passes the ... 3 ... usually sits ... today she is sitting ... 4 I rarely
carry ... I am carrying one ... 5 What do you generally do ...?
6 Are you enjoying ...? 7 Do you enjoy ...? 8 We nearly always
spend ... 9 ... usually sells ... this week he is selling ... 10 Do
you wash ...? 11 ... generally begins ... and is cooking now ...
12 She is still sleeping ... usually wakes ... 13 Why are you wearing
...? I never wear one ... 14 Joan is still doing ... who always works
quicker, is already playing ... 15 ... generally build ... They are
working ... 16 What are you doing ...? If you aren't doing anything ... 17 ... who is studying ... 18 ... generally comes ...
he is visiting ... 19 Do you often watch ...? ... is installing ...
20 ... usually wears ... as the sun is shining, she is not wearing one.

EXERCISE 76

1 Do you see ...? 2 Are you listening ...? Do you understand me?
3 I notice Mary is wearing ... 4 She doesn't understand what you
mean. 5 I need ... They are offering ... 6 Do you smell gas? I
think ... 7 She is drinking ... she hates it. 8 John seems ... 9 It
is still raining, but it looks ... 10 Do you mind helping me ...? I am
trying ... 11 .... what he wants. 12 Do you remember the name
... is walking ...? 13 ... I prefer beer ... 14 I suppose .... My
wife is waiting ... 15 Do you see ...? It contains ... 16 ... who
resemble ... are studying art ... 17 ... do you really mean ... you
still believe him? 18 Do you suppose the children are still sleeping?
19 ... is still standing ... Do you think ...? 20 I notice you pos-
sess ...

EXERCISE 77. As example.

EXERCISE 78. As example.

EXERCISE 79

1 The Jones family are going . . . 2 Are you going . . .? 3 John is
selling . . . and buying . . . 4 . . . I am catching . . . 5 . . . I'm coming
soon. 6 . . . Our guests are leaving . . . 7 . . . I'm shopping . . . and
having lunch . . . 8 We are visiting . . . and spending . . . 9 . . . film
is coming . . . 10 . . . I am playing tennis . . .

EXERCISE 80

1 When do you return . . .? 2 I get back . . . 3 At what time does
your plane take off? 4 . . . party set off . . . 5 . . . we leave . . . stay one
night . . . and return . . . 6 John gets back . . . 7 . . . company em-
bark . . . 8 . . . and the ship sails . . . 9 The manager flies . . . 10 . . . to
hear you leave so soon.

EXERCISE 81

1 They have just arrived . . . 2 They have still not succeeded . . . 3 I
have this very minute received . . . 4 We have already had . . . 5 I
have now studied . . . 6 They have been living . . . 7 We have been
waiting . . . 8 They have already rung . . . 9 . . . you have just had
. . . 10 She has been writing . . . but I have not started . . . 11 The
children have been sleeping . . . 12 How long have you been staying
. . .? 13 They have been working . . . 14 Since when have you had
. . .? 15 I have been knocking . . . 16 They have been building . . .
17 I have tried . . . and have been . . . 18 . . . have you been . . .?
19 He has been going . . . 20 He has taken . . . and has failed . . .
21 William has married . . . 22 I have been trying . . . 23 She has
just spent . . . 24 He has been working . . . and has just finished . . .
25 Have you ever read . . .?

EXERCISE 82

1 (a) . . . until you promise . . . (b) . . . until you have promised . . .
Etc.

EXERCISE 83

1 . . . froze . . . Etc.

EXERCISE 84

1 I was washing . . . rang. 2 She was sitting . . . came home. 3 He
was watching . . . 4 What were you doing . . .? 5 . . . while John was
mending . . . 6 They were studying . . . 7 . . . when she heard . . .

8 ... when they saw ... 9 ... got hurt. 10 ... was digging ...
11 She was looking ... she had ... 12 I was trying ... 13 ... was
looking ... 14 ... while I was waiting ... 15 She was already lying
... 16 ... but I never found ... 17 ... was already flying ... 18
... He was sitting ... 19 ... while she was spending ... 20 They
were all having ...

EXERCISE 85

1 walked. 2 was walking. 3 was swimming. 4 swam. 5 was cooking.
6 cooked. 7 were driving. 8 drove. 9 did not wear. 10 was wearing.
11 Did you often play ...? 12 She was playing ... 13 mended.
14 was mending. 15 talked. 16 was talking. 17 baked. 18 were
flying. 19 was working. 20 was just getting out.

EXERCISE 86

1 He told me ... had never met ... 2 They wanted ... what had
happened. 3 I knew that they hadn't been ... 4 He said he hadn't
been ... 5 She believed that she had put it away ... 6 I was told that
the plane hadn't left ... 7 We wondered if he had lost ... 8 I
couldn't remember whether he had paid ... 9 ... believed that they
had already done ... 10 Did you really think that he had been thrown
...? 11 John wanted to know why Mary had come ... 12 He was
... that they had made ... 13 She was unable ... where she had got
... 14 They told me they had only once seen ...

EXERCISE 87

1 ... he had already left ... realized he had forgotten. 2 She burst
... the moment he had shut. 3 began ... had cut. 4 lost ... after he
had bought. 5 began ... as soon as he had found. 6 The fire had
burnt. 7 It had already rained ... stepped. 8 already died ...
arrived. 9 entered ... had already escaped. 10 got home, night had
already fallen. 11 Until he had explained ... did not understand.
12 had taken off ... could not hear ... 13 had watered ... they did
not grow. 14 would not speak ... until he had apologized. 15 They
were not able ... had brought.

EXERCISE 88

1 slept. 2 you didn't mention. 3 came. 4 we had not stayed. 5 didn't
always rattle. 6 had not arrived. 7 they had worked. 8 he left. 9
knew. 10 came. 11 had. 12 he had not washed. 13 I did. 14 I had
done. 15 we had done.

SECTION 8. CONDITIONAL SENTENCES

EXERCISE 89

1 have/is. 2 are/go. 3 throw/sinks. 4 has/must. 5 heat/melts. 6 go/must. 7 learn/is. 8 grow/water. 9 sing/am. 10 can/speak.

EXERCISE 90. Free completion.

EXERCISE 91

Nos. 1–18 Simply omit 'If you' at the beginning and insert 'and' 19 Let him escape and he will do . . . 20 Let me have . . . and I'll write . . . 21 Let them come and I'll talk . . . 21 Let us try and we may succeed.

EXERCISE 92. Free completion.

EXERCISE 93. Free completion.

EXERCISE 94

1 . . . or else you'll catch. 2 . . . or else you'll drop. 3 . . . or else you will fail. 4 . . . or else you will cut. 5 Find a seat or else there won't be . . . 6 I must go now or else I shall miss . . . 7 Give me that immediately or else I shall get . . . 8 Hurry or else you'll be . . . 9 Follow the instructions or else you will . . . 10 . . . or it will get . . .

EXERCISE 95

1 saw/would be. 2 asked. 3 would collapse/went. 4 had/would dress. 5 would hear/spoke. 6 Would you marry. 7 would play/had. 8 would serve/spoke. 9 would produce/were improved. 10 he would lend/asked. 11 wanted/would have to get. 12 tried/could. 13 would propose/gave. 14 would taste/had. 15 were (was)/would not say.

EXERCISE 96

1 Were he to listen OR If he were to listen. 2 Were that man to take OR If that man were to take. 3 Were I ever to hear OR If I were ever to hear. 4 . . . were we to study OR if we were to study. 5 . . . were he to write OR if he were to write. 6 Were the lecturer to speak OR If the lecturer were to speak. 7 Were we to climb OR If we were to climb. 8 . . . were he to drink OR if he were to drink. 9 . . . were I to buy OR if I were to buy. 10 Were you to meet OR If you were to meet. 11 Were he to present himself OR If he were to present. 12 Were he to enter OR If he were to enter. 13 . . . were it to stop OR if it were to stop. 14 Were I to become OR If I were to become. 15 Were the plane to crash OR If the plane were to crash.

EXERCISE 97. Free completion.

EXERCISE 98

1 they had not come. 2 should never have understood. 3 would have been. 4 had had. 5 had known. 6 would have fought. 7 had not been tied. 8 would have played/had not rained. 9 would have given. 10 had studied/would have passed. 11 had known. 12 would have missed/had not huғried. 13 had not stopped. 14 had eaten. 15 had fallen/would have drowned.

EXERCISE 99. Free completion.

EXERCISE 100. Free completion.

EXERCISES 101, 102 AND 103. Free completion.

SECTION 9. PREPOSITIONS

EXERCISE 104

1 at; 2 in; 3 since; 4 in; 5 at; 6 at/in; 7 since; 8 for; 9 on/at; 10 from; 11 by; 12 by; 13 by; 14 in; 15 for; 16 since; 17 at; 18 at; 19 on; 20 by; 21 on; 22 by; 23 since; 24 in; 25 in; 26 on; 27 since; 28 since; 29 at; 30 in; 31 on; 32 for; 33 at; 34 since; 35 on; 36 on; 37 from; 38 from; 39 since; 40 from.

EXERCISE 105

1 for/since; 2 for/since; 3 since/since; 4 since/for; 5 for/since; 6 since/(for); 7 for/since; 8 for/since; 9 for/since; 10 for/since.

EXERCISE 106

1 over; 2 below; 3 under; 4 over; 5 under; 6 above/under; 7 above; 8 above; 9 under; 10 under; 11 over; 12 above; 13 below; 14 under; 15 beneath; 16 under(neath); 17 below; 18 above; 19 beneath; 20 under; 21 over; 22 below; 23 over; 24 above OR below; 25 below; 26 over; 27 under; 28 under; 29 above; 30 under; 31 under; 32 under; 33 over; 34 under (beneath).

EXERCISE 107

1 among; 2 between; 3 among; 4 between; 5 among; 6 among; 7 among; 8 among; 9 between; 10 between; 11 among; 12 between; 13 between.

EXERCISE 108

1 at; 2 in; 3 at; 4 in; 5 at/in; 6 in/in; 7 at; 8 in/in; 9 in/at;
10 at; 11 at/in; 12 at; 13 in; 14 at; 15 in/in; 16 in.

EXERCISE 109

1 to; 2 towards; 3 for; 4 towards/against; 5 for; 6 at; 7 to; 8
at; 9 at; 10 at; 11 at; 12 for; 13 for; 14 towards; 15 towards;
16 against; 17 to; 18 to; 19 at; 20 against.

EXERCISE 110

1 out of; 2 off; 3 out of; 4 from; 5 of; 6 of; 7 from; 8 off; 9
off; 10 off; 11 from; 12 from/off; 13 off; 14 from; 15 from;
16 of; 17 from; 18 of; 19 from/from; 20 of/of.

EXERCISE 111

1 with; 2 of; 3 of; 4 in; 5 in; 6 with; 7 in; 8 with; 9 with;
10 in; 11 of; 12 in; 13 of/in; 14 of/in; 15 of; 16 with; 17
with; 18 in/with; 19 with; 20 in/with.

EXERCISE 112

1 at table. 2 at a loss. 3 at that. 4 At all events. 5 at the same time.
6 At times. 7 at sight. 8 at work. 9 at war. 10 at will. 11 At first.
12 at play. 13 at table. 14 at most. 15 at last. 16 At first sight. 17
at a profit. 18 at times. 19 at heart. 20 at once. 21 at all costs. 22
at hand. 23 at a pinch. 24 at a moment's notice. 25 at sea.

EXERCISE 113. Free composition.

EXERCISE 114

1 by mistake. 2 by day/by night. 3 By good fortune. 4 by design.
5 by sight. 6 you by name. 7 by yourself. 8 by far. 9 by mistake
(accident). 10 by cable. 11 by far. 12 by chance. 13 by mistake.
14 by no means. 15 by all means. 16 by rights. 17 by degrees. 18
by the way.

EXERCISE 115. Free composition.

EXERCISE 116

1 in common. 2 in fun. 3 in difficulties. 4 in the end. 5 in sight.
6 in pieces. 7 in place. 8 in tears. 9 in a sense. 10 in ink/in pencil.
11 in a way. 12 in brief (short). 13 in all. 14 in particular. 15 in
need. 16 in itself. 17 in debt. 18 in that case. 19 in some way. 20 in
all likelihood. 21 in a hurry. 22 in turn. 23 in trouble. 24 in the
long run (in the end). 25 in due course. 26 in the end.

EXERCISE 117

1 on purpose. 2 on business. 3 on duty. 4 on the other hand. 5 on foot. 6 on the whole. 7 on a visit to. 8 on sale. 9 on fire. 10 on guard. 11 on pleasure. 12 on leave. 13 on a journey. 14 on holiday. 15 on horseback. 16 on duty. 17 on my account. 18 on any account. 19 on second thoughts. 20 on the whole.

EXERCISE 118

1 out of work. 2 out of sight. 3 out of danger. 4 out of order. 5 out of use. 6 out of control. 7 out of doors. 8 out of stock. 9 out of reach. 10 out of the question. 11 out of date. 12 out of breath. 13 out of hearing. 14 out of turn. 15 am out of practice.

EXERCISE 119

1 on time. 2 At one time. 3 by that time. 4 before my time. 5 For a time. 6 at that time. 7 at a time when. 8 behind the times. 9 to time. 10 in time. 11 one at a time. 12 Once upon a time. 13 time after time. 14 In times of. 15 At times. 16 at the time. 17 for the time being.

EXERCISE 120. Free composition.

EXERCISE 121

1 to; 2 at; 3 at; 4 at; 5 to; 6 to; 7 at; 8 to; 9 at; 10 at; 11 at; 12 to; 13 to; 14 to; 15 to; 16 at; 17 to; 18 to; 19 to; 20 at; 21 at; 22 to; 23 at; 24 to; 25 to; 26 to; 27 at; 28 at; 29 at; 30 to; 31 at; 32 to; 33 to; 34 to; 35 to; 36 at; 37 to; 38 at; 39 to; 40 to; 41 to; 42 to; 43 to; 44 at; 45 to; 46 to.

EXERCISE 122

1 of; 2 with/for; 3 of; 4 of; 5 of; 6 of; 7 with; 8 for; 9 with; 10 of; 11 of; 12 with; 13 for; 14 of; 15 of; 16 with; 17 for; 18 of; 19 of; 20 with; 21 for; 22 of; 23 with; 24 for; 25 of; 26 with; 27 for; 28 of; 29 with; 30 for; 31 of; 32 with; 33 for; 34 of; 35 with; 36 of; 37 for; 38 of; 39 for; 40 of; 41 of; 42 of; 43 for; 44 of; 45 of.

EXERCISE 123

1 from; 2 in; 3 on; 4 about; 5 in; 6 from; 7 in; 8 on; 9 about; 10 from; 11 about; 12 in; 13 from; 14 about; 15 on; 16 about; 17 about; 18 from; 19 in; 20 about; 21 in; 22 from; 23 about; 24 about; 25 about.

EXERCISE 124

1 at; 2 to; 3 at; 4 at; 5 to; 6 at; 7 to; 8 at; 9 to; 10 to; 11
to; 12 to; 13 to; 14 to; 15 at; 16 to; 17 at; 18 to; 19 to; 20 to;
21 at; 22 to; 23 to; 24 to; 25 at; 26 to; 27 to; 28 to; 29 at;
30 to; 31 to; 32 at; 33 to; 34 at; 35 to; 36 to; 37 at; 38 to;
39 to; 40 to; 41 at/to; 42 to; 43 at; 44 to; 45 at; 46 to; 47 to;
48 to; 49 to; 50 to.

EXERCISE 125

1 on; 2 in; 3 on; 4 on; 5 in; 6 on; 7 on; 8 on; 9 in; 10 on;
11 on; 12 on; 13 on; 14 in; 15 on; 16 on; 17 on; 18 in; 19 on;
20 in; 21 in; 22 on; 23 on; 24 in; 25 on; 26 on; 27 on; 28 on;
29 in; 30 on; 31 in; 32 on; 33 in; 34 on; 35 in; 36 on; 37 in;
38 in; 39 on; 40 in; 41 on; 42 on; 43 in; 44 on; 45 on; 46 on.

EXERCISE 126

1 of; 2 from; 3 from; 4 from; 5 of; 6 of; 7 of; 8 from; 9 of;
10 of; 11 from; 12 from; 13 of; 14 from; 15 from; 16 from;
17 of; 18 from; 19 of; 20 of; 21 from; 22 from; 23 of; 24 from;
25 of; 26 of; 27 from; 28 of; 29 from; 30 from; 31 of; 32 from;
33 from; 34 of; 35 of; 36 of; 37 from; 38 of; 39 from; 40 of;
41 from; 42 of; 43 of; 44 from; 45 from.

EXERCISE 127

1 for; 2 with; 3 against; 4 against; 5 for; 6 with; 7 with; 8
with; 9 for; 10 with; 11 for; 12 for; 13 against; 14 with; 15
with; 16 with; 17 for; 18 for; 19 with; 20 against; 21 with; 22
for; 23 against; 24 with; 25 for; 26 for; 27 with; 28 against;
29 for; 30 with; 31 for; 32 with; 33 with; 34 with; 35 against;
36 with; 37 for; 38 with; 39 for; 40 for/for; 41 for; 42 with;
43 with; 44 for; 45 with; 46 with; 47 for; 48 for; 49 with; 50
for; 51 against; 52 with; 53 for; 54 for; 55 with; 56 against;
57 for; 58 with; 59 with; 60 with; 61 for.

EXERCISE 128

1 of; 2 with; 3 for; 4 on; 5 to; 6 about; 7 in; 8 from; 9 beside
(between) etc.; 10 at; 11 to; 12 at; 13 on; 14 for; 15 past; 16
over; 17 with; 18 up; 19 to; 20 behind; 21 of; 22 to; 23 for;
24 after; 25 about; 26 by; 27 to; 28 to; 29 at; 30 about; 31 at.

EXERCISE 129

1 They will not come until they are . . . 2 I did not manage to do it
until you had . . . 3 They did not take a liking to the beer until they

tasted . . . 4 I shall not go to bed until I have finished . . . 5 The maid will not open the door until she knows . . . 6 John did not wake up until he heard . . . 7 We will not leave until the other guests have . . . 8 He did not arrive until Wednesday . . . 9 John did not get back . . . until very late. 10 The bus does not leave until all the places are . . .

1 It was not until I paid . . . 2 It was not until three o'clock that . . . 3 It was not until he saw . . . 4 It was not until they tasted . . . 5 It was not until she had read . . . 6 It was not until it was . . . 7 It was not until he came . . . 8 It was not until the children had finished . . . 9 It was not until that Sunday morning that . . . 10 It was not until the seventeenth century that . . .

SECTION 10. PHRASAL VERBS AND ADVERB PARTICLES

EXERCISE 130

In this exercise there are various alternatives. 1 back, round; 2 up, back, along; 3 away, out, about; 4 away, back; 5 along, past; 6 down, back; 7 past, along; 8 off, away; 9 in; 10 up, back; 11 away, off; 12 over, across; 13 over, down; 14 down, over, across; 15 through; 16 up/off, in/out; 17 off, away; 18 on, away, back; 19 over, in; 20 round; 21 away; 22 over, across; 23 along, about, around; 24 past, by, over; 25 across; 26 in; 27 through; 28 on, off; 29 away; 30 off.

EXERCISE 131

(1) *Alternatives are possible in this exercise.* 1 drove; 2 sailed; 3 march; 4 came; 5 went; 6 ran; 7 swam; 8 come; 9 rushed.
(2) 1 drink; 2 used; 3 wind; 4 packed; 5 torn; 6 washing; 7 dried; 8 cutting; 9 wakes; 10 sweeping; 11 saved; 12 wrap; 13 fill; 14 buttoned; 15 locked; 16 do.

EXERCISE 132

(1) 1 pulling; 2 tearing; 3 fall; 4 knock; 5 cut; 6 break; 7 burnt; 8 tone.
(2) *Alternatives are possible.* 1 copy; 2 get; 3 write; 4 put; 5 set.

EXERCISE 133

(1) 1 set; 2 called; 3 read; 4 speaking; 5 shouted; 6 marking; 7 draw; 8 copied; 9 write OR copy.

(2) 1 broke; 2 broke; 3 burst OR broke; 4 burst.

(3) 1 wash; 2 faded; 3 gave; 4 worn; 5 go; 6 put; 7 rubbed 8 wiped; 9 dying; 10 turn.

(4) *Alternatives are possible.* 1 paid; 2 shared; 3 give; 4 handed; 5 given; 6 divided.

(5) 1 stick; 2 point; 3 hung; 4 stretch; 5 jutted; 6 held; 7 stick; 8 hold; 9 stretch; 10 reach.

EXERCISE 134

(1) *Alternatives are possible.* 1 set; 2 going; 3 cool; 4 died; 5 drove; 6 flew; 7 pass; 8 hurried; 9 went; 10 switch; 11 wear.

(2) 1 get; 2 fall; 3 blown; 4 slipped; 5 jumped; 6 knocked; 7 tumbling.

EXERCISE 135

(1) *Alternatives are possible.* 1 keep; 2 go; 3 come; 4 hurried; 5 drive; 6 keep; 7 carry; 8 read; 9 keep; 10 went.

(2) *Alternatives are possible.* 1 hang; 2 stick/nail; 3 pinned; 4 fix OR stick; 5 switch; 6 turn; 7 sewn; 8 put; 9 nailed; 10 hang; 11 screw.

EXERCISE 136

1 thinking; 2 read; 3 talk; 4 read; 5 looked; 6 look; 7 go.

EXERCISE 137

When repeating the exercise with pronouns: 1 Put them up. 2 woke him up. 3 pulling it down. 4 take it off. 5 heated it up. 6 Hold it out. 7 keep it down. 8 lifting it up. 9 thought it over. 10 write them down. 11 sticking them on. 12 rub it out. 13 knocked him down. 14 read it out. 15 gave it all away.

EXERCISE 138

1 In came the Christmas pudding ... 2 ... and off blew his hat. 3 ... and down fell all the books. 4 ... and away ran the deer ... 5 ... and out it fell ... 6 ... and up came the whale ... 7 Down he jumped ... 8 ... and on he went ... 9 ... but on they struggled ... 10 ... but in he fell ... 11 Out you go! 12 ... but back they came ... 13 Along they came ... 14 Off they went ... 15 ... and round swung the great ship.

EXERCISE 139

To put one's hat on
to put back your handkerchief
to put back a book on the shelf
to keep the cat in
to let the cold in
to switch the radio on
to pull someone back
to bring his plate back
to build the pile of bricks up again
to lie down in bed
to let down the cover
to close down an office
to get off a bus
to take some money out

to hand in the books
to warm the engine up
to tear the label off
to take down a notice
to put down one's hand
to pull in your tongue
to walk away from the door
to take something back
to build the house up
to jump back over the stream
to sit down in one's chair
to stick the stamp on
to pull the knob out
to get up onto your horse
to climb over
to stand up again
to straighten up again

EXERCISE 140

1 up; 2 up; 3 out; 4 up; 5 for; 6 up; 7 out; 8 without; 9 off;
10 up; 11 in; 12 with; 13 out; 14 off; 15 up; 16 up; 17 over.

EXERCISE 141

1 up; 2 about; 3 out; 4 off; 5 on; 6 off; 7 by; 8 round; 9 out;
10 upon; 11 across; 12 round; 13 about; 14 round.

EXERCISE 142

1 off; 2 out; 3 in; 4 off; 5 on; 6 in; 7 up; 8 off; 9 out/on;
10 in; 11 away; 12 through; 13 back; 14 off; 15 out; 16 down.

EXERCISE 143

1 down; 2 up; 3 out; 4 through; 5 away; 6 over; 7 over; 8
about; 9 on; 10 on; 11 down; 12 through; 13 about; 14 to; 15
past; 16 back; 18 out OR in; 19 at; 20 on; 21 away.

EXERCISE 144. For explanation.

EXERCISE 145

1 out; 2 down; 3 up; 4 off; 5 out; 6 over; 7 on; 8 off; 9 at;
10 up; 11 down; 12 off; 13 on; 14 down; 15 up.

EXERCISE 146

1 in; 2 to; 3 through; 4 on; 5 out; 6 off; 7 out; 8 off; 9 up;
10 upon; 11 up; 12 in; 13 off; 14 out; 15 in.

EXERCISE 147

1 up; 2 up; 3 off; 4 out; 5 out; 6 in; 7 up; 8 down; 9 out;
10 out; 11 about; 12 down; 13 to; 14 away; 15 on; 16 out.

EXERCISE 148

1 out; 2 to; 3 in; 4 over; 5 up; 6 up; 7 on; 8 in; 9 out; 10
off; 11 up; 12 to; 13 down; 14 out; 15 after.

EXERCISE 149

1 off; 2 out; 3 off; 4 out; 5 up; 6 out; 7 out; 8 off; 9 up;
10 up; 11 up; 12 up; 13 out; 14 out; 15 off; 16 up; 17 up;
18 off.

EXERCISE 150

1 onrush; 2 outburst; 3 outcast; 4 outgoing; 5 downfall; 6 off-
chance; 7 outspoken; 8 downtrodden; 9 income; 10 onset; 11
bygone; 12 outstretched; 13 downpour; 14 outlay; 15 upheaval;
16 downcast; 17 outcry; 18 outbreak; 19 uplifted; 20 downcast;
21 onlookers; 22 oncoming; 23 by-pass; 24 outlook; 25 output;
26 intake; 27 outlet; 28 outset.

EXERCISE 151

1 setback; 2 set-to; 3 set-up; 4 hangers-on; 5 goings-on; 6 take-
off; 7 stand-by; 8 send-off; 9 come-down; 10 wash-out; 11 get-
away; 12 write-up; 11 drawback; 14 throw-out; 15 cast-off; 16
mix-up; 17 worn-out; 18 look-out; 19 run-through; 20 try-out;
21 talking-to; 22 dropping-off.

EXERCISE 152. For explanation.

EXERCISE 153. Free composition.

SECTION 11. PUNCTUATION

EXERCISE 154

1 . . . hot day(!). 2 . . . silly of him(!). 3 . . . on earth is this(?). 4
Hullo(!). 5 No matter(!). 6 How many have you(?) What(!) Twenty-
three(!) Oh well(!). 7 Hush(!) Do be quiet(!). 8 . . . you've made of
it(!). 9 . . . you're doing(?). 10 . . . you are(!) . . . have you been(?).

11 Good Lord(!). 12 Who's there(?). 13 Congratulations(!) . . . getting married(?). 14 . . . happy returns(!). 15 your bicycle(?). 16 . . . is it(?) . . . give me another(?). 17 ——. 18 ——. 19 What(!) . . . arrived yet(?) . . . shall we do(?). 20 ——. 21 Bother(!). 22 ——. 23 Bad luck(!) . . . try again(?). 24 Shut up(!). 25 . . . it's lost(!) . . . shan't we(?).

EXERCISE 155

1 (,) who is in Paris(,). 2 (,) who is a nurse(,). 3 to Paris(,) where. 4 ——. 5 bicycle(,) which. 6 Mr. Smith(,) who. 7 ——. 8 my garden(,) which. 9 ——. 10 George(,) who . . . fisherman(,) is. 11 Mr. Roberts(,) whose. 12 ——. 13 Dee(,) where we. 14 ——. 15 Botany(,) which.

EXERCISE 156

1 he comes(,) give him. 2 ——. 3 ——. 4 before he came(,) we were. 5 ——. 6 ——. 7 ——. 8 you go(,) you see these. 9 If I were you(,) I shouldn't. 10 I was tired(,) I didn't. 11 ——. 12 as you hear(,) let us. 13 his brother(,) I should. 14 as it may(,) I shall not. 15 ——. 16 are rich(,) there is no need. 17 ——. 18 consent(,) I shall. 19 ——. 20 ——. 21 ——. 22 ——. 23 ——. 24 was over(,) they all. 25 choose(,) you must.

EXERCISE 157

1 (,) softly . . . door(,). 2 The game . . . over(,). 3 Turning my head(,) I could. 4 (,) seeing us . . . cards(,) went. 5 (,) made . . . mahogany(,) was. 6 (,) I may say(,). 7 (,) found . . . counts(,) was led. 8 (,) untouched by . . . manufacture(,). 9 (,) surrounded . . . admirers(,). 10 (or,) failing that(,) send. 11 they(,) supposing . . . true(,) threw. 12 (,) my . . . neighbour(,). 13 (,) as you can see(,). 14 (,) the youngest . . . family(,). 15 (,) whether . . . or not(,). 16 (,) whatever . . . say(,). 17 (,) the weather . . . cold(,). 18 The sun . . . set(,). 19 (,) footsore and weary(,). 20 (,) once stopped(,).

EXERCISE 158

1 his coat(,) straightened his tie(,) and dusted off his shoes(,) John. 2 so angry(,) frustrated(,) and. 3 (,) air or rail(,) you must. 4 Standing or sitting(,) eating or drinking(,) sleeping or waking(,) my dog. 5 Slowly(,) carefully(,) and with . . . caution(,) he raised. 6 Cups(,) saucers(,) plates(,) dishes(,) all. 7 of man(,) solitary(,) poor(,) nasty(,) brutish(,) and short. 8 (,) including judge(,) jury(,) public(,) and lawyers(,). 9 books(,) papers(,) magazines(,) and letters. 10 Nearer and nearer(,) louder and louder(,) and . . . insistent(,).

EXERCISE 159

1 I(,) however(,) have. 2· They all(,) nevertheless(,) agreed. 3 Here(,) now(,) is. 4 What(,) then(,) must I do. 5 Where(,) for heaven's sake(,) are you. 6 That(,) in brief(,) is the plan. 7 He was(,) naturally(,). 8 You must(,) of course(,) ask your. 9 have one(,) too. 10 I don't like it(,) though. 11 He decided(,) understandably(,) that it. 12 My wife has(,) for a long time(,) been. 13 They have(,) quite unjustifiably(,) closed. 14 This(,) for what it is worth(,) is my plan. 15 The maid(,) without . . . permission(,) took.

EXERCISE·160

Semi-colons advised in Nos. 1, 3, 4, 5, 6.

EXERCISE 161

1 Colon after 'first'. 2 Colon after 'rules'. 3 ——. 4 Colon after 'do'. 5 Colon after 'I want'. 6 ——. 7 Colon after 'in this way'. 8 Colon after 'have'. 9 ——. 10 Colon after 'telephone'.

EXERCISE 162

1 (')Never(!) (') he said(.) (')I shall never agree to that(.)(')
2 (')What on earth(,)(') he asked(,) (')are you doing(?)(')
3 (')It only costs fivepence(,) (') he said(.) (')Would you like one(?)(')
4 (')Give it to me immediately(,)(') he demanded(.)
   (')No(,)(') she replied(,) (')I refuse(.)(')
5 (')Would you(,) if I asked you(,)(') he asked(,) (')lend me your car(?)(')
6 (')I'll see you later(,) then(.)(')
   (')Not too late(,) please(,)(') she asked(.)
7 (')I'll see you later(,)(') he said(,) and put down the receiver(.)
8 (')Good Heavens(,) no(!)(') she cried(.) (')That's quite impossible(.)(')
9 (')Can you believe it(!)(') said Joan(.) (')He actually asked me to marry him(.)(')
10 (')When(?)(')
   (')Now(.)(')
   (')Where(?)(')
   (')To my house(.)(')
   (')All right(.) If you wish(,)(') he agreed(.)

EXERCISE 163

1 (T)he day after (C)hristmas, (G)eorge called on the (M)ayor.
2 (Y)ou can cross the (T)hames at (W)estminster to visit the (H)ouses of (P)arliament.
3 (I) started to learn (G)erman in (J)anuary last year.

4 (R)obert wants to become a colonel before his brother, the (M)ajor.

5 (I)s (S)ir (W)illiam a knight or a baronet?

6 (T)he (S)wiss have been expert watchmakers since the (M)iddle (A)ges.

7 (K)ings and queens are mortal; so are emperors and empresses.

8 (O)thello, the (M)oor of (V)enice, is a play of (S)hakespeare's.

9 (K)ant's (C)ritique of (P)ure (R)eason is one of the . . .

10 (T)homas is flying to (R)ome by (B.O.A.C.) on the (T)hursday after (E)aster.

SECTION 12. SPELLING

EXERCISE 164

multiplying	obeying	employing	marrying
multiplied	obeyed	employed	married
terrifying	praying	burying	delaying
terrified	prayed	buried	delayed
enjoying	drying	frying	trying
enjoyed	dried	fried	tried
playing	prying	modifying	supplying
played	pried	modified	supplied
qualifying	studying	destroying	replying
qualified	studied	destroyed	replied
straying	displaying	swaying	annoying
strayed	displayed	swayed	annoyed
conveying	denying	betraying	purifying
conveyed	denied	betrayed	purified
hurrying	relying	spraying	allying
hurried	relied	sprayed	allied

EXERCISE 165

merriment	payment	boyish	greyer
enjoyable	funnily	enjoyment	carriage
marriage	joyous	employment	beautiful
plentiful	faultily	glorious	drily

bodily
cloudiness
jollier
burial
trial
sixtieth
stickiest
undeniable

sleepiness
ignominious
merrily
studious
saltiness
jolliest
various

payable
furious
multiplication
betrayal
greasiness
alliance
joyful

prayer
annoyance
thirtieth
layer
reliable
variable
victorious

EXERCISE 166

monkeys
turkeys
furies
babies
follies
aunties
berries

supplies
chimneys
valleys
bodies
dormitories
ways

cries
days
stories
glories
victories
laboratories

replies
donkeys
storeys
joys
sympathies
jellies

EXERCISE 167

multiplies
betrays
prays
employs
hurries
sways
marries
fries

buries
relies
strays
buys
worries
annoys
stays
dries

plays
cries
solidifies
modifies
enjoys
jellies
qualifies
conveys

replies
flies
denies
tries
supplies
displays
terrifies

EXERCISE 168

bigger
winner
rubber
humming
patter
sagged
runner
muddy

beggar
robber
sitting
shrugged
wettest
hatter
batting
uppish

running
hidden
letting
slammed
stepping
fittest
warrior

hottest
riddance
whipped
nagging
betting
potter
sunny

EXERCISE 169

admittance
beginning
conferred
loyalist
pardonable

regrettable
offered
omitted
considering
upsetting

committed
happening
entering
repellant
compelling

prosperous
visitor
murderer
interring

EXERCISE 170

sweeten	cheapen	boiling	wooden
golden	rotten	hotter	longest
rooted	feeding	budding	setting
seating	betted	beaten	fallen
waiter	sweater	ridden	reading
ripping	reaping	leanest	thinnest
witty	parted	lasting	faster

EXERCISE 171

impel	well	kiss	fizz
whizz	fell	if	hell
buzz	stiff	barrel	pill
rebel	bell	peril	damsel
parcel	compel	miss	morsel
kernel	kennel	sell	jewel
still	instil	distil	this
fill	fulfil	analysis	feel
stuff	staff	leaf	

EXERCISE 172

weak	wick	wreck	lock
fantastic	prick	trick	seek
lick	rock	rook	knock
lack	panic	frolic	colic
tonic	took	book	emphatic
stock	public	plastic	frock

EXERCISE 173

fill	feel	pill	peel
refill	tall	avail	appal
travel	appeal	seal	sill
until	tassel	pull	repel
till	pool	well	fulfil
bowel	vowel	towel	duel

EXERCISE 174

appalled	jeweller	duelist	cancelling
repealed	rebellious	stealing	bedevilled
snivelled	impelled	unfeeling	befouled
repellant	libellous	traveller	drivelling
fulfilled	tunnelled	available	fulfilment
pedalled	failure	disembowelling	railing

EXERCISE 175

prizing	loving	continuing	inclining	rhyming
prized	loved	continued	inclined	rhymed
tiring	dining	mining	saving	voting
tired	dined	mined	saved	voted
naming	firing	smiling	reviling	behaving
named	fired	smiled	reviled	behaved
abating	shaming	hoping	coping	faring
abated	shamed	hoped	coped	fared
confiding	praising	razing	blazing	facing
confided	praised	razed	blazed	faced
	raking	using	raging	
	raked	used	raged	

writer	wiry	praiseworthy	behaviour
wisely	ninety	movement	lovable
noiseless	noisy	hopeless	continual
tiresome	lovely	shameful	razor
abatement	removal	arrival	disposal
pleasure	inflation	hygienic	believable
useful	movable	composition	catalogued
saviour	revolved	fertility	

advantageous	serviceable	managed	manageable
replaceable	gracious	peaceable	irreducible
aging	ageless	tracing	embraced
judgement	enlargement	engaging	disparagement
spicy	enticing	conducive	knowledgeable
courageous	replacing	outrageous	indulgent
abridgement	plunging	arranging	

EXERCISES 176 AND 177. For reading and dictation.

EXERCISE 178

(a) *Long vowels*

wine, wave, alive, rose, rove, game, drove, drive, tome, derive, behave,
shave, tone.

(b) *Short vowels*

give, have, dove, gone, shone, above, one, surface, done, live,* some
forgive, glove, come, preface, love, become, handsome, liver.

Note: * The adjective 'live' would be in list (a).

EXERCISE 179. For dictation.

EXERCISE 180

abandon	accident	adept	adhere	affection
abominable	accent	acrobat	addition	affair
abbreviate	accept	abundant	address	affirm
abolish	accommodate	accumulate	adjust	adore
accurate	accompany	achieve	admire	adverse
access	according	academy	admit	adopt
account	aggravate	alone	altogether	afford
afflict	agenda	alarm	alteration	ammonia
afar	aggression	allegiance	always	although
alliance	already	almighty	afraid	agriculture
allure	allow	almost	anatomy	appetite
ammunition	announce	appear	approximate	apology
apparatus	apostle	appendix	amount	appointment
apartment	applaud	appeal	arrange	assent
attach	attain	attempt	arouse	assemble
attend	attitude	atom	arrest	assign
attribute	atrocious	assure	arithmetic	assume
astonish			arable	
eclipse	economy	eccentric	editor	educate
effect	efficient	effort	elephant	emolument
essay	essence	establish	estate	esteem
dissatisfy	disappear	disservice	disown	disability
dimish	disapprove	disengage	dispatch	disease
dissect	dissimilar	display	displease	dissolve
distribute		disuse		
illegal	illiterate	illusion	illustrate	idle
ignite	ignorant	imagine	imitate	immature
immediate	immense	immoral	immune	immortal
inedible	inelastic	inequality	innocent	innumerable
inoffensive	irregular	inorganic	irresistible	irresponsible
irritate		irony	irrelevant	
political	police	pollute	polygonal	possess
possible	positive	position	possessive	
obvious	obliterate	obedient	obscure	occasion
occupation	occur	ocean	offend	official
ommission	onion	opportune	oppose	opinion
oppress	optician			

substitute	subtract	success	succumb	summary
summit	superb	support	supplement	suppose
surety	supreme	surrender	survey	survive
supply	sudden			

EXERCISE 181

wharves (also -fs)	leaves	wives	knives	loaves
roofs	proofs	beliefs	hoofs (also -ves)	reefs
sheaves	chiefs	briefs	lives	halves
calves	strifes	selves	reliefs	gulfs
shelves	wolves	safes		

EXERCISE 182

volcanoes	tomatoes	potatoes	photos	pianos
solos	heroes	allegros	cargoes	echoes
oratorios	octavos	haloes	negroes	radios
ratios	shampoos	tangos	kangaroos	mementos (also
mosquitoes	torpedoes			-oes)

EXERCISE 183. For pronunciation.

EXERCISE 184. For dictation.

EXERCISE 185

1 [au]	drown	row	allow	brow
	sow	bow	gown	now
	cow	vow	brown	crown
	fowl	owl	crowd	frown
				clown
2 [ou]	row	snow	blow	low
	sow	bow	crow	follow
	throw	slow	flow	show
	hollow	fellow	bestow	below
	bowl	grow	glow	

Note: These words have both pronunciations but with different meanings: row, sow, bow.

EXERCISE 186

1 [o:]	source	pour	port	floor
	sword	more	torn	course
	storm	north	cork	forth
	fourth	wore		
2 [ə:]	worth	courtesy	journey	work
	worse	colonel	worm	worst
	world			

EXERCISE 187

1 [o]
common	cloth	wrong	pot
bomb	doll	across	rot
upon	shop	cough	donkey
gong			

2 [ʌ]
some	son	one	cover
Monday	above	colour	love
blood	come	glove	London
shove	dove	tongue	thorough
brother	honey	none	monkey
among	mother		

EXERCISE 188

sheep	weep	deem	seek
keel	heap	deep	seen
deed	wheat	leap	peel, peal
keen	heed	feet, feat	heat
weal, wheel	heel, heal	bead	fleet
seat	peak	reed, read	sleep
reap	beat	leak, leek	meal

EXERCISE 189. For dictation.

EXERCISE 190

1 long 'u' [u:]
	soothe	stoop	loot
fool	food	roof	room *
smooth	boon	tool	mood
moon	goose	tooth	pool
cool	spoon	shoot	

2 short 'u' [u]
room	book	cook	good
wood	soot	shook	look
took	hood	wool	hook

Note: * is a variant pronunciation.

EXERCISE 191

1 [i:]
wheat	seat	sea	lead
read	pea	clean	bean
dream	lean	league	breathe
steal	heap	treat	

2 [e]   lead   dead   stead   deaf
        weapon   dread   breast   breath
        dreamed   leaped   leaned   bread
        threat

Note: The word 'lead' has both pronunciations with a different meaning for each; 'read' in the present tense = [ri:d] but in the past tense = [red].

EXERCISE 192

1 [u]   push   pull   butcher   cushion
        bull   pudding   bush   full
        sugar   bullet   bulletin fulfil
        pulpit   pussy   put

2 [ʌ]   rush   gull   hutch   Russian
        dull   budding   hush   lucky
        Sunday   funny   pulse   fussy
        but

EXERCISE 193

1 [ou] foal   float   though   road
        goal   moan   goad   mould
        goat   shoal   shoulder boulder
        load

2 [o:] soar   boar   board   source
        hoarse   mourn   hoard   court
        pour   roar   ought

EXERCISE 194

1. 1 [ə:] first   third   girl   fur
            heard   earth   pearl   earn
            journey   work   courtesy firm
            burn   worm   world   word
            fir   turn   worst

    2 [a:] star   Derby   heart   clerk
            far

    3 [o:] more   door   soar   court
            ward   warn   war   shore
            warm

2.   1 [iə]   hear   fear   here   ear
               beard   beer   steer   mere
               tier   austere   clear   dear
                                       peer

     2 [eə]   bare   hair   where   air
               pare   their   bear   stair
                           there   pear
                                       stare

     3 [uə]   doer   endure   cure
               poor   fewer
               sure   bluer
               truer

EXERCISE 195

knave (nave)	need	knead	net	knife
knight (night)	nought	knit	neat	knob
nub	knock	know (now)	knuckle	nickel
knew (new)	newer	knell	knot (not)	naked
knickers	nib	nymph		

lamb	dram	gum	rum	thumb
bomb	comb	drum	rim	limb
jam(b)	clam	climb	cram	succumb
groom	numb	slim	slum	womb
hum	dumb			

almond	walk	stalk	salmon	should
bake	could	revoke	half	palm
sham	psalm	calm	ram	safe
folk	yolk	coke	talk	ham
behave	behalf	chalk	halve (have)	would

sign (sin)	resign (resin)	campaign	sovereign	main
design	foreign	reign (rein)	strain	pain
benign	feign	disdain	complain	malign

write (rite)	wrong	wrap (rap)	wrist	rate
rip	wrest (rest)	wretched	wrinkle	wring (ring)
wreck	root	ran	wren	rope
wry	wrote	wrath	rut	wriggle
rely	rank	rune	rob	run

fasten	hasten	listen	whistle	lessen
wrestle	tassel	castle	lesson	mussel
fissile	gossip	apostle	passing	chasten
vassal	vessel	christen	fossil	thistle
missal	rustle	rissole	mistletoe	kissing

EXERCISE 196

rage	badge	ledge	edge	age
lodge	baggage	luggage	porridge	deluge
subterfuge	gouge	siege	hatch	witch
brooch	approach	couch	pouch	slouch
patch	peach	beech	fetch	wretch
gauge	match	besiege	ditch	refuge
knowledge	cottage	stitch	catch	huge
stage	teach	judge		

EXERCISE 197. For dictation.

EXERCISE 198

classroom	armchair	raincoat	bookcase
school-teacher	reading-lamp	teaspoon	headmaster
riding-school	bookshop	boot polish	boy scout
history master	housewife	waistcoat	forehead
blue-eyed	saucepan	flagstaff	horse-racing
motor-car	telephone box	watercolour	post-war
international	pro-Belgian	co-operation	co-existence
bank-note	hospital bed	penknife	cupboard
handwriting	sea-shore	nonsense	non-intervention
post-natal	floodlit	countryman	pre-Shakespearian
dining-room	bathroom	gaslight	writing-paper
notepaper	milk jug	letter-box	camp-bed
sitting-room			

SECTION 13. WORD BUILDING

EXERCISE 199

nightly	elderly	soldierly	daily
friendly	ghostly	daughterly	yearly
scholarly	sugary	womanly	hourly
rascally	Godly	oily	muddy
cloudy	sunny	kingly	fortnightly
maidenly	windy	misty	snowy
grassy	beastly	watery	earthy
silky	rubbery	silvery	rusty

EXERCISE 200

1	boyish	clownish	swinish
monkish	amateurish	devilish	slavish
brutish	sheepish	mulish	waspish
sluggish	kittenish	selfish	

2	Spanish	Frankish	Moorish
	Finnish	Polish	

3	strongish	stiffish	longish
softish	greyish	youngish	poorish
	stand-offish		tightish

EXERCISE 201

warlike	cumbersome	wearisome	trustworthy
handsome	fulsome	wholesome	noisome
irksome	troublesome	childlike	cowlike
lovesome	ladylike	statesmanlike	workmanlike
seamanlike	Christlike	fearsome	rodlike
blameworthy	quarrelsome	doglike	noteworthy
awesome	respectworthy	seaworthy	airworthy
roadworthy	paperlike	loathsome	burdensome
meddlesome	lifelike	businesslike	lonesome

EXERCISE 202

responsible	bearable	reasonable	convertible
considerable	changeable	foreseeable	debatable
accessible	defensible	respectable	suitable
admirable	readable	divisible	contemptible
regrettable	valuable	permissible	avoidable

EXERCISE 203

inacceptable	unreasonable	unreadable	incomparable
inadmissible	unthinkable	unprintable	inaccessible
indefensible	unbelievable	unbeatable	indefinable
unbearable	ineligible	undesirable	undependable
unusable	unworkable	unteachable	indigestible
unpalatable	indifferent	unpronounceable	unclimbable

EXERCISE 204

{ unsatisfied { dissatisfied	disapprove	uncomfortable	untrustworthy
disappear	disbelieve	distrust	disappoint
inconvenient	discomfort	disarmament	disagree
displease	disoblige	{ uncover { discover	disfavour
disgrace	{ disgraceful { ungraceful	discourage	dishonest
disobey	disorder	{ dissoluble { insoluble	inapplicable
unfortunate	infamous	inappropriate	{ unconnected { disconnected
inefficient	infrequent	inconsiderable	inequality
disloyal	{ unlike { dislike	inconclusive	unequal
unfavourable	discreditable	unbelievable	unkind

EXERCISE 205

mistaken	misinformed	misapplied	{ distrusted { mistrusted
misjudged	discontinued	mislaid	misread
disinclined	disaffected	{ misplaced { displaced	misshapen
mistranslated	{ misused { disused	{ miscounted { discounted	misled
disliked	misspelled	misunderstood	discovered
disordered	displeased	misappropriated	disinherited
misdirected	misconstrued	misleading	

EXERCISE 206

List I		List II		List III
with -less only		with -less and -ful		with -ful only
water	penny	harm	meaning	truth
tree	sleep	use	taste	success
child	time	help	rest	forget
sound	price	purpose	pain	mind
cease		joy	regard	play
hair		thank	heed	beauty
eye		care	thought	
base		need	colour	
sense		fruit		

EXERCISE 207

These adjectives require 'more' and 'most' to form their comparatives and superlatives. The remainder form them with -er and -est.
brutish, beautiful, regular, elderly, interesting, capable, thorough, real modest, frequent, evil, difficult, curious, content, childish, splendid.

EXERCISE 208

1 wind-swept; 2 tailor-made; 3 snow-covered; 4 college-trained; 5 silver-plated; 6 candle-lit; 7 rubber-soled; 8 tree-lined; 9 hand-knit(ted); 10 horse-drawn; 11 black-eyed; 12 quick-witted; 13 bad-mannered; 14 coffee-coloured; 15 long-haired; 16 well-dressed; 17 well-spoken; 18 hard-hearted; 19 well-stocked; 20 leather-covered.

EXERCISE 209

1 fire-eating; 2 fast-moving; 3 time-consuming; 4 quick-growing; 5 high-flying; 6 long-suffering; 7 grass-cutting; 8 water-purifying; 9 quick-firing; 10 slow-running.

EXERCISE 210

1 three-hour; 2 three-hundred mile; 3 fivepence; 4 four-thousand foot; 5 four-hand; 6 four-gallon; 7 four-storey; 8 five-finger; 9 two-hundred page; 10 fourteen-stone; 11 fourteenth-century; 12 second-class; 13 three-year; 14 fourth-year; 15 18-horse-power.

EXERCISE 211

1 sound-proof; 2 waterproof; 3 ill-gotten; 4 matter-of-fact; 5 never-to-be-forgotten; 6 long-drawn-out; 7 ready-to-wear; 8 well-thought-out; 9 ill-fitting (or badly-); 10 weather-beaten; 11 up-to-date; 12 so-called; 13 day-to-day; 14 out-and-out; 15 uncalled-for; 16 down-to-earth; 17 long-suffering; 18 red-handed; 19 made-to-measure; 20 well-informed.

EXERCISE 212

1 over-tired; 2 over-ripe; 3 under-done; 4 over-dressed; 5 over-exposed (or under-); 6 under-paid; 7 under-populated; 8 overrated; 9 underfed; 10 over-anxious; 11 over-confident; 12 over-fond; 13 overcrowded; 14 under-manned; 15 over-careful; 16 under-developed.

EXERCISE 213

wisdom	freedom	princedom	librarianship
ladyship .	scholarship	showmanship	lordship
championship	girlhood	knighthood	maidenhood
relationship	officialdom	manhood	curatorship
brotherhood	fellowship	governorship	sisterhood
parenthood	seamanship	motherhood	childhood
companionship	salesmanship	womanhood	nationhood
likelihood	leadership	partnership	sainthood
spinsterhood	livelihood	martyrdom	horsemanship
fatherhood	bachelordom	hardship	

EXERCISE 214

List B.

beauty	honesty	courage
certainty	generosity	bravery
density	expense	jealousy
safety	danger	patience
difficulty	pride	length
height	intelligence	

EXERCISE 215

flight	death	width	growth	thrift
youth	length	breadth		frost
height	weight	sight	depth	stealth
heat	truth	gift	filth	theft
warmth	birth	drought		

EXERCISE 216

liberator	liar	leader	lawyer
sailor	governor	visitor	decorator
singer	donor	orator	translator
caterer	dancer	officer	scholar
murderer	warrior	Berliner	geographer
golfer	Londoner		
New Yorker	owner		

EXERCISE 217

motorist	pianist	machinist	bicyclist
musician	tobacconist	tourist	Christian
electrician	mathematician	historian	archaeologist
botanist	politician	Parisian	terrorist
apologist	accompanist	Italian	cartoonist
theologian	scientist	artist	Communist
Argentinian	physicist	psychiatrist	
	physician	economist	

EXERCISE 218

employee	absentee	referee	lessee
auctioneer	electioneer	refugee	profiteer
mountaineer	pamphleteer	engineer	
charioteer			

EXERCISE 219

adventuress	seamstress	murderess	tigress
woman cook	shepherdess	heiress	hostess
lioness	sorceress	duchess	princess
traitress	woman violinist	woman speaker	governess
empress	woman singer	paintress	waitress
mistress	woman teacher	mayoress	woman doctor
woman dentist	woman lawyer	actress	conductress

EXERCISE 220. As example.

EXERCISE 221

1 He has overstated his case. 2 to overwind your watch. 3 to under-rate your opponent. 4 after overdosing himself with. 5 has overslept again. 6 He has overspent his allowance. 7 She has overcooked this meat. 8 don't overfill that glass. 9 have overpraised that book. 10 go on undereating. 11 underestimate the building costs. 12 who undercharges his customers. 13 who always overfurnish. 14 to avoid underexposing

EXERCISE 222

strengthen	roughen	shorten	horrify	certify
deepen	widen	pacify	justify	harden
loosen	tighten	solidify	clarify	sanctify
heighten	lessen	liquefy	simplify	falsify
lighten	terrify	stupefy	emulsify	mystify
sharpen	beautify	identify	exemplify	countrify
nullify	intensify	thicken		fatten

EXERCISE 223

hospitalize	sympathize	circularize	specialize	plasticize
regularize	captivate	equalize	pasteurize	commercialize
immunize	pressurize	activate	apologize	rubberize
tranquillize	domesticate	familiarize	satirize	

EXERCISE 224

In these verbs the prefix re- has largely lost its meaning of repeating the action.

recover	reflect	reduce	repair	restore
refute	regard	rejoice	recount	remark
revolve	resist	react	resolve	rehearse
renounce	relax	reveal		

If a hyphen were placed after the re-, the following verbs would have the meaning of repeating the action:–

re-store	re-count	re-mark	re-act	re-solve
re-cover				

EXAMPLE 225

1 He outlived. 2 He outplayed. 3 Children outgrow. 4 outweigh the disadvantages. 5 His competitors outbid him. 6 outlast the soles. 7 outmanoeuvred their opponents. 8 they had outwitted the police. 9 not to be outdone. 10 outjumped all other.

EXERCISE 226

1 upbringing   upheaval   upkeep   to uproot   downcast
  downhearted downfall   upright downpour   downtrodden
  to upholster   uproar

2 outcast   outspoken   outbreak   outburst   ⎰income
  outset   ⎰output   inborn   outcry   ⎱outcome
  ⎰outlay   ⎱input   outfit
  ⎱inlay   ⎰outlet
             ⎱inlet

3 overflow   to overhang   ⎧to under-   oversight   to under-
                           ⎨ take   stand
                           ⎩to overtake to over-   to undergo
             underwear   whelm
  to under- undergrowth   to under-
    mine   line
             undersigned   to over-   to under-   to overlook
                             come   write

4 ⎰offset   onlooker   **onrush**   offspring   offshoot
  ⎱onset   offprint

EXERCISE 227. For this exercise, consult a dictionary.

EXERCISE 228

energy	hypothesis	expanse	explain
athlete	machine	describe	compel
aesthete	music	intensify	illusion
hygiene	divide	attend	sense
publicize	centralize	explode	inflame
diplomat	regiment	defend	confirm
history	occasion	educate	deride
proliferate	colonize	distinguish	refraction
sympathize	continue	deceive	respire
lethargy	form	nominate	defame
relevance	expect	circle	peculiarity
hesitate	militate	family	singularity
obey	penitence	regularize	insularity
suffice	reluctance	similarity	consul
	efficiency	popularity	rectangle
courage	joy	capacity	ferocity
curiosity	righteousness	courtesy	hideousness
voracity	fable		

EXERCISE 229

encrust	encourage	enable	bemoan	
enslave	embitter	enclose	entangle	
entrust	befriend	becalm	enforce	
embolden	enlighten	entitle	belittle	
benumb	besiege	enrich	enrage	bestir
bewitch	ensure	enjoy	enlarge	endanger

EXERCISE 230

breath	bath	loss	choice	loan
belief	use	sale	stroke	song
relief	seat	speech	food	thought
life	strife	advice	blood	abode
half	proof			grief

EXERCISE 231

cartage	refusal	arrival	disposal	dispersal
reversal	approval	breakage	trial	denial
bestowal	passage	demurrage	proposal	package
haulage	marriage	recital	usage	wreckage
betrayal	stoppage	shrinkage	dotage	postage
renewal	leakage	wastage	dismissal	storage
burial				carriage

EXERCISE 232

development	selection	confinement	termination
fulfilment	revolution	discouragement	imprisonment
forbearance	assistance	attendance	government
information	combination	contentment	requirement
resentment	acknowledg(e)ment	confirmation	deliverance
residence	reliance	resignation	cancellation
prediction	refinement	amazement	revelation
commitment	invention	resistance	disappearance
alliance	concealment	embarkation	definition
separation	limitation	presentation	postponement
interference	confidence	endurance	remittance
improvement	investment	devotion	enrichment
arrangement	situation	embankment	occurrence
performance	inheritance	hindrance	

EXERCISE 233

semi-official	semi-detached	non-member	non-intervention
non-combatant	semicircle	non-existent	bipartisan
non-stop	non-aggression	bi-monthly	bi-weekly

inter-college	intercontinental	international	interracial
semi-civilized	semi-final	inter-university	

post-(pre-)war	post-date	postgraduate	post-(pre-)natal
post-(pre-)re-	counterproposal	counterattack	counteract
formation	pre-arranged	pre-existence	post-(pre-)Shake-
countercharge	anticlimax	anti-slavery	spearian
prehistoric	anti-semitic	antibody	pre-Christian
anti-aircraft			post-operative

co-exist	co-operate	co-education	co-, sub-, ex-director
ex-minister	ex-President	coincidence	ex-service man
co-, ex-, sub-	subway	sub-committee	sublet
editor			
subnormal	sub-tropical	demobilize	decentralize
decipher	decarbonize	depopulated	co-workers

EXERCISE 234

household	daybreak	headmaster	workday
henhouse	birthday	master list	workshop
country house	pay-day	master key	work-box
housewife	day school	schoolmaster	needlework
housework	day-time	masterpiece	stonework

tableland	bedroom	time bomb	riverside
kitchen table	hospital bed	night-time	bedside
table tennis	bedclothes	dinner time	side-table
bedside table	hotel bed	timetable	sideboard
table manners	bedstead	time-keeper	side view
bookcase	night-light	water rat	head office
bookseller	lighthouse	waterway	figurehead
reading-book	lightship	sea water	head-dress
account book	lamplight	water-wheel	headman
bookstall	daylight	drinking-water	masthead
music room	hour-glass	looking-glass	newspaper
music stand	dinner-hour	glass-cloth	paper-knife
chamber music	hour hand	eyeglass	paper money
music hall	concert hour	glass paper	writing-paper
piano music	working hour	wineglass	paper bag
walking-shoe	merchant ship	mankind	tableland
shoe-horn	battleship	workman	fatherland
shoemaker	sailing-ship	policeman	landmark
horseshoe	shipyard	manhole	landlord
shoelace	shipbuilder	manslaughter	landslide
towel horse	oil paint	money-box	training-school
cavalry horse	paintbrush	paper money	day school
horseman	water paint	money-lender	schoolmaster
horseshoe	paintbox	blood-money	grammar school
horse-race	paint-shop	money-changer	schoolboy
country road	workshop	clothing factory	floor-space
branch road	bookshop	factory whistle	floor-board
crossroad	shop assistant	factory manager	floor covering
side-road	shop window	cigarette factory	dance-floor
road-mender	hat shop	factory building	threshing-floor
	insurance office	knife-blade	
	office boy	knife-handle	
	office hours	breadknife	
	head office	paper-knife	
	office work	knife edge	

EXERCISE 235

1 seaman; 2 policeman; 3 night-watchman; 4 gentleman; 5 horse-
man; 6 headman; 7 statesman; 8 chairman; 9 milkman; 10
clergyman; 11 fisherman; 12 countryman; 13 railwaymen's; 14
firemen; 15 workmen.

EXERCISE 236

1 sheep-stealing; 2 Cigarette-smoking; 3 cattle-breeding; 4 tobacco-growing; 5 film-making; 6 Mountain-climbing; 7 bull-fighting; 8 trout-fishing; 9 Piano-playing; 10 doll-making; 11 walking-stick; 12 teacher-training college; 13 letter-writing; 14 climbing-boots.

SECTION 14. WORDS

EXERCISE 237

1 puff and pant; 2 splutter; 3 yawn; 4 cough and sneeze; 5 stutter and stammer; 6 sniff; 7 snore.

EXERCISE 238

1 slip; 2 slide; 3 staggered; 4 limped; 5 steal; 6 scrambled; 7 stumbled; 8 hopped; 9 crawl; 10 linger; 11 sprang; 12 crept; 13 prowling.

EXERCISE 239

dog: {snarl and howl; bark and growl.} horse: neigh. cat: purr and mew. hen: cackle and cluck. bee: buzz. cow: low. sheep: bleat. pig: grunt. donkey: bray. frog: croak. snake: hiss. duck: quack. cock: crow. sparrow: chirp and twitter.

EXERCISE 240

1 glare; 2 flickers; 3 glistens; 4 glows; 5 twinkles; 6 shining; 7 sparkled; 8 flashes; 9 gleaming; 10 glimmer; 11 shimmers; 12 glint; 13 dazzled.

EXERCISE 241

1 crash; 2 creaked; 3 cracked; 4 squealed; 5 rattled; 6 slam; 7 roar; 8 rustled; 9 hum; 10 ticked; 11 pealed; 12 tinkled; 13 rumbled; 14 thud; 15 hiss; 16 squeak; 17 clattered.

EXERCISES 242, 243, 244 and 245. For explanation.

EXERCISE 246

1 poured; 2 trickled; 3 spurted; 4 squirting; 5 gushed; 6 drips; 7 spouting; 8 dribble; 9 streamed.

EXERCISE 247

pay a visit	break a promise	keep one's word
work a miracle	catch a cold	catch a train
bear a child	change one's mind	use force
beg pardon	draw a conclusion	wear a look
blow a trumpet	blow one's nose	fall in love
keep one's temper	put a stop to	pay a compliment
serve a purpose	catch fire	lay the table
fly a flag	reach an agreement	throw a glance
waste time	save trouble	drive a bargain
play a trick	lend a hand	play the piano
set free	strike a match	blow up a tire
break a habit	say a prayer	call a meeting
pay attention	earn a living	lose heart
set sail	send word	hold a meeting
keep count of	have occasion to	pay one's respects
fall asleep	tell the time	tell a lie
put to death	turn a corner	have mercy on
catch sight of	pass an exam	ask questions
set fire to	miss a chance	keep a secret
speak the truth	strike the hour	lead a busy life
shake hands	fall ill	run a risk
run a business	put an end to	lose confidence in
lose touch with	tell the truth	set an example
throw light on	find fault with	throw suspicion on

EXERCISE 248

The following words form expressions with 'make':

haste	a mistake	war	enquiries
way	a discovery	a journey	fun of
certain	a choice	good	an escape
one's way	a trip	room for	one's apologies
friends	a face	a complaint	use of
love	excuses	money	peace
repairs	a confession	welcome	an offer
fast			

Note 'repairs' is also found with 'do'.

EXERCISE 249

The following words form expressions with 'take':

shape	notice of	breath	pleasure in
leave of	place	an interest	examinations
a holiday	pains	pride in	root
fright	hold of	care	flight
offence	turns	a photograph	a liking to
steps to	pity on	charge of	

EXERCISE 250

In this exercise 'go' can only be used in Nos. 3, 4, 6, 8, 9, 12, 16, 20.
'grow' cannot be used in Nos. 6, 7, 10, 17, 19, 20.
'get' cannot be used in Nos. 6, 20.

EXERCISE 251

1 Fetch, bring; 2 take; 3 carry; 4 take; 5 carry; 6 take; 7 fetch; 8 Bring, fetch; 9 bring; 10 take; 11 carry; 12 fetch; 13 brought; 14 fetched; 15 carried; 16 Take; 17 fetch; 18 brings; 19 Take carry; 20 takes.

EXERCISE 252

1 raise; 2 rose; 3 raise; 4 rose; 5 raised; 6 rose; 7 raise; 8 raise; 9 risen; 10 lying; 11 lie; 12 laid; 13 lain; 14 lying; 15 lie; 16 laid; 17 lay; 18 laid; 19 lying; 20 Lay.

EXERCISE 253

1 tell; 2 saying; 3 say; 4 tell; 5 say/tell; 6 say; 7 tell; 8 say; 9 said; 10 say; 11 tell; 12 telling; 13 tell; 14 tell; 15 tell; 16 tell; 17 say; 18 tell; 19 saying; 20 tell; 21 tell.

EXERCISE 254

1 Fires started in many. 2 His knowledge of English is improving. 3 The new headmaster and his staff will meet. 4 A stone dropped into. 5 His plane flew low. 6 The baby leaned against. 7 The patch stuck firmly. 8 The house shook. 9 The door shut behind. 10 The metal bar bent at its. 11 The pictures are hanging. 12 His pen broke when he. 13 The children must not wake. 14 The parties should divide into three. 15 The ship sailed eastwards. 16 Their English vocabulary increases every year. 17 My hand hurts. 18 When are John and Mary going to marry? 19 The cradle is rocking. 20 The ball rolled. 21 The bat swung through. 22 Flags waved when. 23 The door opened and John walked. 24 All the children collected. 25 The crowd kept moving along. 26 ... if the projector would work. 27 The rope stretched from. 28 The water poured onto the. 29 The children kept dry by. 30 Her opinion of him never changed. 31 The engine turned over and. 32 All the people were gathering together in the.

EXERCISE 255

1 Mr. Smith grows vegetables in his garden. 2 The soldiers stood their rifles. 3 The captain sank the ship. 4 The manager ran the business. 5 They must freeze the water. 6 He quickly burnt the paper. 7 The teacher will begin the lesson. 8 You must boil the water. 9 Has the maid cooked the meat yet? 10 Please pass the wine round the table.

EXERCISE 256

1 I do hope. 2 and am expecting. 3 I am definitely not looking forward to. 4 I hope very much. 5 I hope. 6 I expect. 7 always hoping . . . I don't expect. 8 is hoping. 9 I expect so. 10 waiting for? 11 waited . . . expecting. 12 Are you looking forward 13 wait for me. 14 expected. 15 expecting . . . wait for them. 16 waited for. 17 expecting . . . hopes. 18 waiting. 19 I expect . . . not looking forward to it. 20 looking forward . . . I hope . . . and I expect.

EXERCISE 257

1 avoid—prevented. 2 avoid—prevent. 3 avoid—prevent. 4 Avoid —prevented. 5 avoided OR prevented—prevent. 6 avoid—prevent. 7 prevent—avoid. 8 avoid—prevent. 9 avoided/prevent—avoid/prevent. 10 avoid—prevent.

EXERCISE 258

1 They robbed my wife of a valuable ring. 2 Some thieves robbed Mrs. Jones of her handbag. 3 They robbed my house of all the ready cash. 4 The burglars robbed the grocer of £25. 5 The bank was robbed of £5,000 last night. 6 Which house in the street was robbed of those papers? 7 Who was robbed of his wallet? 8 She was robbed of her last penny.

EXERCISES 259, 260, 261, 262 and 263. For vocabulary study.

EXERCISE 264

The following have the same form for the man and his nationality:

Russian	Hungarian	Indian	Cingalese
Lebanese	Brazilian	Norwegian	Portuguese
German	Siamese		Chinese
Greek	Swiss		

The following have two separate forms:

Irishman—Irish	Frenchman—French
Turk—Turkish	Dutchman—Dutch
Pole—Polish	Finn—Finnish
Spaniard—Spanish	Japanese (also a Jap)—Japanese
New Zealander—New Zealand	Welshman—Welsh
Yugoslav—Yugoslav(ian)	Dane—Danish

Scotland has: A Scot or a Scotsman and Scottish or Scotch.

EXERCISE 265

butcher—sells meat; barber—cuts hair; conductor—sells tickets on a bus; judge—administers the law; miner—obtains coal from the ground; newsagent—sells newspapers and magazines; nurse—looks after the sick; porter—carries luggage; tobacconist—sells tobacco; spectator—sees something happen; surgeon—operates on sick people; carpenter—makes chairs and tables; greengrocer—sells fruit and vegetables; painter OR artist—paints pictures; baker—makes bread; journalist OR reporter —writes for the newspapers; sculptor—carves statues; detective—investigates crimes; doctor—cures sick people; policeman—controls traffic; sailor—works on a ship; tourist—travels for pleasure; farmer—cultivates the land; ironmonger—sells metal goods; chemist—sells medicines and drugs; fishmonger—sells fish.

EXERCISE 266

Chairman—committee; Editor—newspaper; Headmaster—school; Chef—kitchen; Foreman—workshop; General—army; Conductor—orchestra; Captain—ship; Pilot—aeroplane; Dean—University Faculty; Judge—Court of Law; Speaker—Parliament; Captain—football team; Housewife—household; Manager—bank; Admiral—navy; President—Republic; Manager—business firm; Leader—party of climbers; Host(ess)—party or reception.

EXERCISE 267

bachelor—spinster; Sir—Madam; drake—duck; landlord—landlady; boar—sow; manservant—maidservant; bridegroom—bride; widower —widow; stallion—mare; king—queen; nephew—niece; monk—nun; wizard—witch; headmaster—headmistress; Boy Scout—Girl Guide; uncle—aunt; hero—heroine; cock—hen; barman—barmaid; bull—cow; gentleman—lady.

EXERCISE 268

calf—cow; kitten—cat; duckling—duck; cub—lion; piglet—pig; chicken—hen; cub—bear; eaglet—eagle; lamb—sheep; puppy—dog; gosling—goose; foal—horse.

EXERCISE 269

Monastery—monk; asylum—lunatic; stable—horse; nest—bird; sty—pig; house—man; convent—nun; cowhouse (cowshed)—cow; shell—snail; tent OR caravan—gypsy; palace—king; barracks OR camp—soldier; kennel—dog; web—spider; prison OR gaol (jail)—convict; cottage—peasant; hive—bee; nest—wasp.

EXERCISE 270

flock of sheep; swarm of bees; pack of cards; fleet of ships; herd of cattle; bundle of old clothes; bunch of keys or flowers; staff—office workers; pair of scissors; flight of steps; crew—sailors and airmen; gang of thieves.

shoal of fish; mob of angry people; crowd of people in the street; audience—people in the theatre; congregation—people in church; chest of drawers; haystack; suit of clothes; set of tools; clump of trees; pair of trousers; bunch of grapes.

EXERCISE 271

milk by the pint; beer by the pint OR bottle; butter by the pound; matches by the box; potatoes by the stone OR sack; coal by the sack; eggs by the dozen; flowers by the bunch; ribbon by the yard; toilet soap by the cake; cigarettes by the packet; tobacco by the ounce; shoes by the pair; sewing cotton by the reel; string by the ball; land by the acre; shaving soap by the stick.

EXERCISE 272

in a packet: cigarettes; in a basket: eggs, flowers, groceries; in a trunk: clothes for a journey; in a tank: liquids of all sorts; in a safe: money, documents and valuable papers; in a tube: toothpaste, paint, glue; in a vase: flowers; a cellar: wine; a purse: money; a kettle: water; a wardrobe: clothes; a briefcase: documents and papers; a can: food and liquids; a cask: wine or beer; an envelope: a letter; a jug: water or milk; a suitcase: clothes and things for a journey; a barrel: beer, water; a bath: water; a flask: water, brandy; a satchel: school books and exercise books; a wallet: money and identification papers; a compact: powder.

EXERCISE 273

telephone number: a telephone directory; the date: a calendar; position of a country: map, atlas; the time of a train: timetable; story of someone's life: biography; old letters in an office: a file; where a name is mentioned in a book: index; the meaning of a word: dictionary; information on a subject: encyclopaedia; list of goods and prices: catalogue; a daily record of personal events: diary; a collection of family photographs: album.

EXERCISE 274

scissors for cutting cloth and paper; saw for cutting wood into planks; hammer for driving in nails; chisel for carving wood; file for making metal smooth; spade for digging in the garden; axe for cutting down trees; plane for making wood smooth; screwdriver for putting in screws; rake for collecting together dry leaves; pliers for holding and bending wire; drill for making holes in wood or metal.

EXERCISE 275

handcuff: criminals; chain: anchor; nails and screws: woodwork; string: parcel; mortar: bricks; zip: dress; pin: brooch; hinge: door; thread: cloth; nuts and bolts: metalwork; clip: paper; strap: trunk; laces: shoes; button: jacket; glue or gum: paper.

EXERCISE 276. Consult a dictionary.

EXERCISE 277

a grain of salt; a speck of dust; a drop of rain; a crumb of bread; a morsel of food; a blade of grass; a chip of wood; a scrap of paper; a lock of hair; a breath of air; a puff of wind; a fragment of pottery.

EXERCISE 278

A.D. (Anno Domini) = in the year of our Lord; used for the years of the modern era since the birth of Christ, e.g. A.D. 1215.

h.p. = horse-power; used to show the power of a machine or car, e.g. 15 h.p.

B.C. = Before Christ, e.g. 55 B.C.

P.T.O. = please turn over; written at the bottom of a page to show that the text continues on the other side.

Messrs. (Messieurs); used when addressing an envelope to a business firm.

a.m. (ante meridiem) = before midday; used to show the hours of the morning.

Mrs. [misiz] only to be used when followed by a name; is not used as a form of address.

St. = Street OR Saint; e.g. Oxford St., St. Paul's Cathedral.

etc. (et cetera) = and the rest; used at the end of a list = and so on.

U.K. = United Kingdom; i.e. England, Scotland, Wales and Northern Ireland.

i.e. (id·est) = that is; used to introduce an explanation.

Co. = company; used in the titles of business firms.

R.S.V.P. (Répondez s'il vous plaît) = please reply; written at the bottom of a formal invitation when a reply is needed.

p.m. (post meridiem) = after noon. See a.m.

e.g. (exempla gratia) = for example; used to introduce an example.

Rd. = Road; used in addresses.

R.N. = Royal Navy; placed after a man's name to show that he is an officer in the Royal Navy.

Esq. = Esquire; only used after the name of a man when addressing an envelope.

U.S.A. = United States of America.

M.P. = Member of Parliament.

do. (ditto) = the same; used when writing a list to avoid repeating the same words with every new item.

Mr. = Mister; only used when followed by a name; see Mrs.

U.S.S.R. = Union of Socialist Soviet Republics.

c/o = care of; used when addressing a letter to someone who is staying in another person's house, e.g. John Smith, Esq., c/o Mrs. Jane Robinson.

Dr. = Doctor.

P.S. (post scriptum) = a post-script; used when you wish to add more to a letter which you have already signed.

Ltd. = limited; used in the names of Limited Liability Companies.

v. (versus) = against; used when announcing the names of two persons or teams taking part in a match, e.g. Bolton Wanderers *v.* Arsenal.

No. = number.

B.B.C. = British Broadcasting Corporation.

U.N.O. = United Nations Organization.

TV = television; used both in writing and speaking [ti : vi:].

EXERCISE 279

1 Mon. Tues. Wed. Thur. Fri. Sat. Sun.

2 Jan. Feb. March. Apr. May. June. July. Aug. Sept. Oct. Noy. Dec.

3 penny = p.; pound sterling = £.

4 sec. min. hrs. yrs.

5 m. yds. ft. ins.

6 oz. lbs.

EXERCISES 280, 281 and 282. For explanation.

EXERCISES 283 and 284. Free composition.

EXERCISE 285

1 The whole family enjoyed. 2 the whole film. 3 the whole school. 4 the whole day. 5 the whole book. 6 the whole cake. 7 during the whole journey. 8 the whole term. 9 the whole exercise. 10 the whole time. 11 The whole room. 12 The whole week. 13 The whole fleet. 14 the whole party. 15 The whole house.

EXERCISE 286

1 He has lost everything. 2 Everybody was. 3 for everybody. 4 by everybody. 5 since everybody is present. 6 everything to me. 7 everything. 8 to which everybody is invited. 9 where everybody can. 10 which everybody can enjoy.

EXERCISE 287

1 fairly; 2 rather; 3 rather; 4 fairly; 5 rather; 6 fairly; 7 rather; 8 rather; 9 fairly; 10 rather; 11 rather; 12 rather; 13 rather; 14 rather; 15 rather.

EXERCISE 288

With the meaning of *completely* with these adjectives:

terrified	illegal	tired out	white
right	different	wrong	helpless
unusual	amazed	sour	
hopeless	extraordinary	useless	inexperienced
black	desperate	outrageous	